Fernanda Baldanza

Human Rights Education

Fernanda Baldanza

Human Rights Education

Strategy for Development as Freedom

ScienciaScripts

Imprint

Any brand names and product names mentioned in this book are subject to trademark, brand or patent protection and are trademarks or registered trademarks of their respective holders. The use of brand names, product names, common names, trade names, product descriptions etc. even without a particular marking in this work is in no way to be construed to mean that such names may be regarded as unrestricted in respect of trademark and brand protection legislation and could thus be used by anyone.

Cover image: www.ingimage.com

This book is a translation from the original published under ISBN 978-613-9-67290-5.

Publisher:
Sciencia Scripts
is a trademark of
Dodo Books Indian Ocean Ltd. and OmniScriptum S.R.L publishing group

120 High Road, East Finchley, London, N2 9ED, United Kingdom
Str. Armeneasca 28/1, office 1, Chisinau MD-2012, Republic of Moldova, Europe
Printed at: see last page
ISBN: 978-620-8-15699-2

SUMMARY

ACKNOWLEDGMENTS 2

SUMMARY 3

1 INTRODUCTION 4

2 literature review 6

3 METHODOLOGY 41

4 RESULTS AND DISCUSSION 43

5 EDUCATIONAL PRODUCT - COURSE PLAN 51

6 CONCLUSION 56

APPENDIX A - SURVEY INSTRUMENT 57

REFERENCES 59

I dedicate this work to all the human rights activists on this planet who, despite facing all kinds of obstacles and violence, resist in the fight for a better world.

ACKNOWLEDGMENTS

To my family, in equal gratitude, for all their love and motivation.

To my friends, for all their patience and understanding.

To my advisor Prof.[a] . Maria Geralda de Miranda, for her teachings, guidance and dedication.

To Prof. Silvia Melo, for her teachings, tenderness and excellence in her classes.

To all the professors of the *Stricto Sensu* Postgraduate Program in Local Development, Prof.[1] . Katia Avellar, Prof. Rodrigo Otâvio Souza, Prof. José Seixas and Prof. Reis Friede, for their teaching and dedication.

To the entire UNISUAM Master's administrative team, for their usual diligence and promptness.

To my classmates, for all the companionship and friendship that made this course more enjoyable and pleasurable.

To everyone who contributed in any way to making this important moment a reality.

In particular, to my grandfathers Hudson Baldanza (*in memoriam*) and Adhemar dos Santos Pinto (*in memoriam)*, to my grandmothers Guiomar Alves Trugano (*in memoriam)* and Juracy Scaramelo Baldanza, to my father Mauro Scaramelo Baldanza, to my mother Alzira Maria dos Santos Pinto, to my sisters Clara Pinto Diniz and Andressa Pinto Diniz, to my nephew Pedro Diniz Reis, to my dear friend Luis Felipe Reis, to my cousin Fernanda Braga Pinto, for the "simple" fact that they exist.

For a world where we are socially equal, humanly different and totally free.

(Rosa Luxemburg)

SUMMARY

We are currently living through one of the most critical moments in human history. The world is experiencing the greatest human suffering since World War II.[a] Just look at the refugee crisis and the endless civil wars in the Middle East. In Brazil, human rights violations occur in practically every area of social life, whether at work, at school, in educational institutions, in everyday life and, above all, on social networks. Waves of intolerance, discriminatory practices, violence, contempt for certain groups, hate speech and, above all, the distortion of the notion of human rights, have contributed to this peculiar moment in national history. Human Rights Education (HRED) has been enshrined in practically all international human rights documents, at first with the aim of publicizing the provisions of the International Covenants and now with the aim of transforming the culture of human rights violations into a culture of respect, recognition and appreciation of the human person. This dissertation assessed the human rights knowledge of the people who attend the Casa do Trabalhador, located in Manguinhos, comprising the group of users who seek legal assistance offered by UNISUAM, through the Manguinhos Project, linked to the Free Legal Assistance and Guidance Program. It was based on the hypothesis that the group's knowledge of human rights was insufficient for them to exercise citizenship. The research was organized in stages, the first being a study on the topic, the second a bibliographical review on human rights and development and in the third, research instruments were applied to the group studied. In the fourth stage, the results were evaluated. In the fifth and final section, as a product of this dissertation, a special HRD program was drawn up, based on the group's main needs. The results indicate that most of the group analyzed had no knowledge of human rights, confirming the hypothesis proposed. Finally, it can be concluded that human rights education is a decisive tool for human transformation and development, as it enables individuals to become subjects of rights who are able to influence the process of development as freedom.

KEYWORDS: Development. Freedom. Human Rights Education.

All men are born free and equal in dignity and rights. They are endowed with reason and conscience and should act towards one another in a spirit of brotherhood.

Art. 1, Universal Declaration of Human Rights - 1948

1 INTRODUCTION

We are all human. The relevance of this (re)affirmation of the nature of the human condition would not be extremely necessary if there were a true culture of peace, respect, tolerance and otherness in the contemporary world. However, the history of humanity has been built and marked by multiple wars and serious violations of human rights.

Although human rights have acquired particular legal and normative expressiveness in recent decades and special protection through the structuring of global and regional protection systems, it is true that the modern world still faces severe forms of outrage against the human person, in its most varied forms, such as the generalization of armed conflicts, the upsurge in violence, the degradation of the biosphere, the growth of ethnic-racial, religious, cultural, territorial, physical-individual, gender, sexual orientation, nationality and political intolerance. (PNEDH, 2007)

The rights internationally recognized by the Universal Declaration of Human Rights, although often violated, are widely disseminated today: right to life, equality, security, justice, protection against all forms of racism and discrimination; freedoms of movement, thought, religious orientation, expression, assembly; right to citizenship and participation in politics and in the cultural sphere of the community; social rights, such as education, work, food, leisure (ALVES, 1999), housing and transportation; right to a dignified existence, right to development, right to a healthy environment, right to peace.

According to Sen (2010), although the contemporary world situation presents undeniable social, technological, economic and political advances, such as changes in the economic sphere, the recognition of democratic and participatory regimes, the emphasis on the concepts of human rights and political freedom, and an increase in life expectancy, today we also live in a world of extraordinary deprivation, destitution, violence and oppression.

According to Sen (2010), overcoming these problems is the central issue of the development process, which aims, above all, to recognize the individual as the central agent of this system, and to consider individual freedom both as a social commitment and as a condition for what Sen calls the expansion of individual capacities. However, individual capacities are limited by the social, political and economic opportunities available to them, establishing the interrelationship between individual freedom and social development.

From this perspective, Human Rights Education is a precise tool in the context of expanding individual freedom by expanding human capacities, because in order to promote and protect any and all rights, we first need to know about them. In this way, only through education that explores the historical, social, political and legal construction of human rights, as well as encouraging students to reflect critically on how violations occur and how to overcome them, will the individual be able to actively participate in the democratic process and be able to influence public policies that recognize, ensure or re-establish human rights while they are being violated.

From this perspective, human rights education seeks to promote development as freedom (Sen, 2010) insofar as it empowers the individual to exercise citizenship and rights, thus expanding their individual capacities and educating for a democratic culture based on the values of tolerance, solidarity, social justice, environmental sustainability, inclusion and plurality (PNEDH, 2007).

This work is divided into five stages. The first stage deals with the theoretical content of Human Rights, Development and Human Rights Education, which are the guiding themes of this research. The second stage shows the methodology used to develop this work. In the fourth stage, the results and discussion of the data obtained were presented. In the final stage, a human rights education course plan was drawn up based on the content covered and with the help of the data obtained.

2 LITERATURE REVIEW

2.1 HUMAN RIGHTS

In recent human history, no expression has been more privileged to bear the mission and weight of humanity's destiny than [the expression] "human rights" [...] - the greatest gift of classical and contemporary human thought is the notion of human rights. In fact, more than any other moral language available at this time in history is the language of human rights.

(BENEDEK, 1994).

2.1.1 Foundations of Human Rights

An important issue to be observed and contextualized initially lies in the delimitation of the foundation of human rights: the human being.

According to the evolutionary thinking of Charles Darwin (1871), the human being is a living being that has evolved like all other species and has a pre-existing ancestor, and is therefore not a metaphysical creation or invention.

In order to explain the evolution of human physical traits, Darwin (Op. Cit.) used the mechanism of sexual selection, whereby members of one sex compete for the attention of the opposite sex, thereby increasing reproductive success. Human intelligence evolved by natural selection as a consequence of upright posture, which freed human hands for the use of tools (ERICKSON et al., 2015).

Karl Jaspers (1965) teaches that man has been defined as a living being endowed with speech and thought, who provides society with the form of a city governed by laws. He also produces tools and uses them for work, and his subsistence is ensured through community planning.

Peter Singer (1993) gave the term human being a punctual and reductionist meaning, stating that they are members of the species Homo Sapiens.

From an existential analytical approach, Pequeno (2012) considers that the human being has six dimensions of existence: biological, psychological, economic, social, cultural and political. It is understood at this point that to these must be added the legal dimension of the human being, as determined by the Civil Code of 2002 in its Article 2: "The civil personality of the person begins with birth; but the law shall safeguard, from conception, the rights of the unborn. "

Comparato (1997, p. 10) believes that the basis of validity of human rights is none other than man himself, considered in his substantial dignity as a person. The Universal Declaration of Human Rights (UDHR, 1948) in its initial article enshrines this premise by stating that: *"All human beings are born free and equal in dignity and rights. "*

In an attempt to define an ontological specificity for human rights today, Comparato (1997, p. 22) draws on modern philosophical anthropology to establish five characteristics of the human being, namely: freedom, self-consciousness, sociability, historicity and the existential uniqueness of the human being.

Freedom is the ability of human beings to act freely without being driven by the voracity of their instincts, because they are the only beings endowed with will. Self-consciousness is the awareness of one's own subjectivity and of one's condition as a living and mortal being (COMPARATO, 1997). In turn, sociability reveals the essentially sociable nature of human beings, as Aristotle teaches (2002, p. 11):

So man is a civic animal, more social than bees and other animals that live together. Nature, which does nothing in vain, has only given him the gift of speech, which should not be confused with the sounds of the voice. These are only the expression of pleasant or unpleasant sensations, which other animals are capable of, like us. Nature has given them an organ limited to this sole purpose; we, however, have more, if not developed knowledge, at least the obscure feeling of good and evil, of useful and harmful, of just and unjust, objects for the manifestation of which we have mainly been given the organ of speech. This trade in words is the bond of every domestic and civil society.

Comparato (1997) also states that human beings only develop their potential as people - their capacity for culture and self-improvement - when they live in society.

With regard to historicity, the author emphasizes that human nature is historical and lives in perpetual transformation, through the memory of the past and the project of the future.

Finally, existential uniqueness presupposes that each human being is unique and irreplaceable in the world, with dignity as an intrinsic characteristic (COMPARATO, 1997), a theme that will be revisited in greater detail in the course of this work.

After the discovery of DNA in 1953 - the genetic material (genome) that contains the crucial information for heredity (ARIAS, 2004) - the existential uniqueness of the human being was contemplated with scientific discoveries. The basis of fundamental human unity was internationally recognized by the Universal Declaration on the Human Genome (UNESCO, 1997, p. 7), which states:

The human genome is the basis of the fundamental unity of all members of the human family, as well as their inherent dignity and diversity. In a symbolic sense, it is the heritage of humanity.

Therefore, the foundation of human rights is the existence of man himself as a human being, so human rights serve to ensure that man exercises his freedom, preserves his dignity and protects his existence (life) (PEQUENO, 2012).

2.1.2 Concept of Human Rights

The legal concept of human rights can be extracted from Resolution No. 1/2012 of the CNE/CP (National Education Council, 2012) in its art. 2, §2, which reads as follows:

Human rights, internationally recognized as a set of civil, political, social, economic, cultural and environmental rights, whether individual, collective, transindividual or diffuse, refer to the need for equality and the defence of human dignity.

According to André de Carvalho Ramos (2014), human rights consist of a set of rights considered indispensable for a human life based on freedom, equality and dignity. For the author, these are the essential and indispensable rights for a dignified life.

Based on a technical legal analysis, Mazzuoli (2015) states that human rights are those guaranteed by rules of an international nature, i.e. by treaties and declarations signed between states with the specific purpose of protecting the rights[1] of people subject to their jurisdiction.

The term fundamental rights is often confused with human rights. As pointed out above, the latter are rights guaranteed by international norms, while the former are rights provided for in constitutional texts, linked to the maximum aspects of protection, in the sense that they are already recognized at the internal level of each State, through contemporary Constitutional Charters. (MAZZUOLI, 2015)

Human rights also have their own characteristics, which were reaffirmed at the Second World Conference on Human Rights in the text of the Vienna Declaration of 1993:

5. All human rights are universal, indivisible, interdependent and interrelated. The international community must consider human rights globally, fairly and equitably, on the same footing and with equal emphasis. While the significance of national and regional specificities and diverse historical, cultural and religious backgrounds must always be borne in mind, it is the responsibility of states, regardless of their political, economic and cultural systems, to promote and protect all human rights and fundamental freedoms.

2.1.3 Historical statement

As Comparato (2003) points out, the most beautiful and important part of human history is the revelation that all human beings, despite the incalculable biological and cultural differences that distinguish them from one another, deserve equal respect. Above all, it is the universal recognition that, because of this radical equality, no one - no individual, gender, ethnicity, social class, religious group or nation - can claim to be superior to others.

This notion of equality and mutual respect between human beings did not emerge at the same time as the discovery of human life on Earth, because, according to Carvalho Ramos (2014), from the first writings of human communities in the 8th century BC to the 20th century AD, more than twenty-

---

1 Internationally recognized rights such as civil and political rights, economic, social and cultural rights, etc.

eight centuries have passed in the course of a universal affirmation of human rights, whose historical milestone is the Universal Declaration of Human Rights in 1948.

Bobbio (2004, p. 5) provides a theoretical foundation based on the historicity of human rights and concludes that these are historical rights, i.e,

born in certain circumstances, characterized by struggles to defend new freedoms against old powers gradually, not all at once and not once and for all.

The author corroborates his theory on the historical relevance of the recognition of human rights based on the following findings:

Religious freedom is an effect of wars and religion; civil liberties, of the struggle of parliaments against absolute sovereigns; Political freedom and social freedoms, from the birth, growth and maturation of the movement of salaried workers, peasants with little or no land, the poor who demand from the public authorities not only the recognition of personal freedom and negative freedoms, but also the protection of work against unemployment, the first rudiments of education against illiteracy, then assistance for invalidity and old age, all of which were needs that rich landowners could satisfy on their own. (BOBBIO, 2014, p. 5)

Based on the theory of historical affirmation, Ramos (2014) also argues that the core of human rights protection is the fight against oppression and the search for the well-being of the individual, focusing his ideas on values such as justice, equality and freedom, whose content has permeated social life since the emergence of the first human communities. Therefore, the process of recognizing values intrinsic to human life has gone through various stages which, over the centuries, have helped to consolidate the concept and legal regime of these essential rights.

It is therefore possible to reconstruct the history of human rights from two different points of view: social history[2] and conceptual history[3] . (TOSI, 2004)

According to the aforementioned authors, history plays a fundamental role in the recognition and protection of human rights, given that new rights are incorporated into human practices as a product of struggles and revolutions, such as the English Revolution (1628), the American Revolution (1776) and the French Revolution (1798).

A very important observation to be made, very well highlighted by Ramos (2014), is to realize that the various phases of evolution of human rights theory have coexisted with institutes or positions that are now repudiated by protection systems, such as slavery, religious persecution, exclusion of minorities, subjugation of women, discrimination against those who are different and autocracy[4]

---

2 It emphasizes the events, struggles, revolutions and social movements that promoted human rights.
3 On the philosophical, ethical, political and religious doctrines that have influenced and been influenced by historical events.
4 According to the *Michaelis* online dictionary autocracy means: *sf (gr autokràteia)* 1 Government exercised by a single

As the basic principles of modern society, human rights have been revealed as ways of fighting against situations of unequal access to material and immaterial goods, discrimination on the grounds of socio-cultural diversity and, in general, oppression linked to the control of power by dominant minorities. (CNE, 2011)

The transformation of these struggles into binding legal norms, based on a culture of rights, has as its milestones the *"Bill of Rights" of* the English Revolutions (1640 and 1688-89); the Virginia Declaration (1776) in the process of emancipation of the 13 colonies from their English metropolis, from which the United States emerged as a nation; the Declaration of Man and the Citizen (1791), in the context of the French Revolution. These three documents affirmed civil and political rights, translated into the principles of liberty, equality and fraternity (CNE, 2011).

[aa]As a result of the tragedies that occurred in the 20th century, beginning with the outbreak of World War I and ending with World War II - which saw the human genocide resulting from the Nazi Holocaust and later the explosion of two atomic bombs in Japan, precisely in the cities of Hiroshima and Nagasaki (CNE, 2011) - the international community sees an urgent need to recognize and protect human rights.

The impact of these atrocities led to the creation of the United Nations Organization in 1945 through the UN Charter, also known as the Charter of San Francisco, which states as much in its preamble:

WE, THE PEOPLES OF THE UNITED NATIONS, RESOLVED

to preserve future generations from the scourge of war, which twice in our lifetime has brought untold suffering to mankind, and to reaffirm faith in fundamental human rights, in the dignity and worth of the human being, in the equal rights of men and women, as well as of nations large and small, and to establish conditions under which justice and respect for obligations arising from treaties and other sources of international law can be maintained, and to promote social progress and better living conditions within a broad freedom.

AND TO THAT END, to practice tolerance and live in peace with one another as good neighbors, and to unite our forces to maintain international peace and security, and to ensure, by the acceptance of principles and the establishment of methods, that armed force will not be used except in the common interest, to employ an international mechanism to promote the economic and social progress of all peoples.[5]

An international organization dedicated exclusively to the recognition, promotion and protection of human rights has emerged in the contemporary world.

The Universal Declaration of Human Rights, proclaimed by the United Nations General Assembly in

---

person, with absolute and unlimited powers. **2 *Sociol*** Discretionary political domination, exercised by one person or a small group of people; it can take the forms of despotism, tyranny, dictatorship and oligarchy, autarchy. (2016) <http://michaelis.uol.com.br/modemo/portugues/index.php?lingua=portugues-   portugues&palavra=autocracia> Accessed on 13/06/2016.
5 UN Charter. Available at <https ://nacoesunidas.org/carta/> Accessed on 27/05/2016.

Paris on December 10, 1948[6] , is the landmark document in the history of human rights. For the first time in the history of humanity, a set of principles and rules establishes the universal protection of these rights, which are recognized as fundamental for a life that guarantees the dignity of the human person.

2.1.4 Generations of Human Rights

The generations of human rights represent the way in which rights have been recognized throughout history. It will be used here to facilitate understanding of the non-hierarchical categories of human rights.

Mazzuoli (2015) teaches that the proposal to triangulate human rights into generations was put forward by Karel Vasak and dates back to the motto of the French Revolution: Liberty, Equality and Fraternity. This order would include first, second and third generation rights.

2.1.4.1 First generation rights (Freedom)

According to Bonavides (2000), the first generation of human rights comprises the rights of liberty and were born with the French Revolution. Barroso (2001) believes that individual rights were born out of the liberal revolutions and are true public freedoms, since they set limits on the actions of power, delimiting the individual's sphere of legal protection from the state. Civil and political rights, based on liberal individualism and aimed at protecting values relating to life, freedoms (movement, expression, assembly, association, conscience, religion, etc.), security and property, are recognized in the International Covenant on Civil and Political Rights (ICCPR - 1966).

2.1.4.2 Second generation rights (Equality)

Second generation rights were born in the 20th century and include equality rights (MAZZUOLI, 2015). As explained by Ramos (2014), they represent a change in the role of the state to adopt an active stance in ensuring minimum material conditions for survival, making the so-called social rights a reality, such as the right to health, education, work, social insurance and housing, listed in the International Covenant on Economic, Social and Cultural Rights (ICESCR - 1966).   1966). These rights require a positive provision from the state in order to be realized.

and are called equality rights precisely because they guarantee the less privileged sections of society the realization of the abstract freedoms previously recognized.

2.1.4.3 Third generation rights

Mazzuoli (2015) teaches that third generation rights are based on the principle of fraternity, and have

---

6 Document available in full on the Universal Declaration of Human Rights website. <http://www.dudh.org.br/wp-content/uploads/2014/12/dudh.pdf> Accessed on 27/05/2016.

been strongly influenced by the environmental issues that emerged in the 1960s. They include the right to the environment, to development, to the common heritage of humanity, to communication, among others.

Among these is the right to development, enshrined by the UN in 1986 in Article 1 of the Declaration on the Right to Development, which is the central theme of this work.

Article 1

1.   The right to development is an inalienable human right, by virtue of which everyone and all peoples are entitled to participate in, contribute to and enjoy economic, social, cultural and political development, in which all human rights and fundamental freedoms can be fully realized.

2.   The human right to development also implies the full realization of the right of peoples to self-determination which includes, subject to the relevant provisions of both International Covenants on Human Rights, the exercise of their inalienable right to full sovereignty over all their natural wealth and resources.

It is also worth highlighting what the American Convention on Human Rights says about development, given its relevance to the subject of this research.

Article 26 Progressive development

The States Parties undertake to adopt measures, both internally and through international cooperation, especially economic and technical, in order to progressively achieve the full effectiveness of the rights deriving from the economic, social and educational, scientific and cultural standards contained in the Charter of the Organization of American States, as reformed by the Protocol of Buenos Aires, to the extent of the resources available, by legislative or other appropriate means.

They are also known as diffuse rights because they are held by an indeterminate plurality of subjects. The United Nations Convention on Climate Change (1992) is an international environmental treaty whose application affects the entire international community.

2.1.4.4 Fourth generation rights

Some authors support the existence of a 4th[a] generation of human rights, which is believed to be entirely plausible due to the technological transformations taking place around the world. Filho (2012) argues that these are rights and guarantees of protection against unbridled globalization and genetic manipulation, the right to democracy, euthanasia, bioethics, biosciences and information technology. These would be the rights of humanity.

2.1.5 . International Protection of Human Rights

2.1.5.1 Axes of international protection

The protection of human rights at international level is concentrated in three specific areas of public international law: International Human Rights Law (IHRL), International Humanitarian Law (IHL), and International Refugee Law (IRL).

These axes are not mutually exclusive, being all integral and constituent parts of the system of international protection of the human being, the last two being intended for special situations, such as armed conflicts (IHL) and the protection of refugees while they are in this condition (DIR), respectively. (MAZZUOLI, 2015)

2.1.5.2 International Protection Systems

A) Universal System

The United Nations Organization (UNO) was created in 1945, as mentioned, and here it is worth highlighting the last paragraph of its preamble:

WE DECIDED TO COMBINE OUR EFFORTS TO ACHIEVE THESE GOALS.

In view of this, our respective Governments, through representatives assembled in the city of San Francisco, having exhibited their full powers, which have been found in good and due form, have agreed to the present Charter of the United Nations and hereby establish an international organization to be known by the name of the United Nations. (UN, 1945)

According to Mazzuoli (2015), the birth of the UN was the real turning point in the process of internationalizing human rights, extending them to all human beings on the planet, which had previously been restricted to a few domestic legislations, such as the English one of 1684, the American one of 1778 and the French one of 1798.

This system is also known as the UN system. Currently, within the scope of UN protection, international treaties and conventions are contemporary sources of human rights. The three reference documents of the international system that make up the International Bill of Human Rights are: the Declaration of Human Rights (UDHR), the International Covenant on Civil and Political Rights (ICCPR) and the International Covenant on Economic, Social and Cultural Rights (ICESCR) (MAZZUOLI, 2015). In addition to these, other international documents make up the universal system in an equally relevant way: Geneva Convention (1949), Convention on the Prevention and Punishment of the Crime of Genocide (1948), Convention against Torture and Other Cruel, Inhuman or Degrading Treatment or Punishment (1984), International Convention on the Elimination of All Forms of Racial Discrimination (1968), Declaration on the Elimination of Violence against Women (1993), Convention on the Rights of Persons with Disabilities (2007), among others.

B) Regional Systems

International law has three regional protection systems: the European, Inter-American and African systems (MAZZUOLI, 2015).

Each system has its own rules and specificities, safeguarding the structuring principle of every human rights system, the dignity of the human person.

2.1.6 Human Rights in Brazil

The Brazilian Federal Constitution of 1988 enshrined in constitutional norms rules and principles that are part of the system of human rights protection. In the view of Carvalho Ramos (2014), human rights have taken center stage in the legal system, the immediate consequence of which is to bind all public powers and private agents to the content of these rights.

To reinforce this understanding, it is important to quote the preamble of the

1988 Constitution:

We, the representatives of the Brazilian people, assembled in the National Constituent Assembly to establish a democratic state, designed to ensure the exercise of social and individual rights, freedom, security, well-being, development, equality and justice as the supreme values of a fraternal, pluralistic and unprejudiced society, founded on social harmony and committed, in the internal and international order, to the peaceful settlement of disputes (...)

The Brazilian Constitutional Charter (1988) also set the following objectives

Article 3 of the Constitution of the Republic calls for the construction of a free, just and solidary society, the guarantee of national development, the eradication of poverty and marginalization and the reduction of social and regional inequalities, as well as the promotion of the good of all, without discrimination of origin, race, sex, color, age or any other form of intolerance, reaffirming the commitment made by the Brazilian State when it signed up to the International Bill of Human Rights.

It also inserts the principle of the dignity of the human person as the foundation and sustaining basis of the Democratic State of Law, revealing the centrality of the human being as the foundation of the entire Brazilian legal and social order.

2.1.6.1 The Dignity of the Human Person

It is based on the principle that the Federal Constitution has chosen the principle of human dignity in Article 3, III, as an essential structuring value for both society and the legal order, as proposed in the preamble to the UDHR (1948):

Considering that the recognition of the inherent dignity of all members of the human family and of their equal and inalienable rights is the foundation of freedom, justice and peace in the world (...)

Art. 1 The Federative Republic of Brazil, formed by the indissoluble union of States and Municipalities and the Federal District, is a Democratic State governed by the rule of law and has as its foundations: III - the dignity of the human person;

According to Sarlet (2015, p. 71) the dignity of the human person can be understood as

the intrinsic and distinctive quality recognized in each human being that makes them worthy of the same respect and consideration by the State and the community, implying, in this sense, a complex of fundamental rights and duties that ensure the person both against any and all acts of a degrading and inhuman nature, as well as guaranteeing them the minimum existential conditions for a healthy life, in addition to providing and promoting their active and co-responsible participation in the destiny of their own existence and of life in communion with other human beings, with due respect for the other beings that make up the web of life.

The dignity of the human person as an essential legal value presupposes a normative content that is difficult to delimit in view of the complexity and breadth of its scope.

We would like to highlight two important theories on the minimum content of human dignity, one by Prof. Luis Roberto Barroso and the other from a recent publication by Prof. Daniel Sarmento.

The recognition of a minimum content for the concept of the dignity of the human person with a universal scope of application is proposed by Barroso (2014) by considering three constituent elements of dignity, but not without first warning that these must be analyzed through the lenses of secularity[7] , neutrality[8] and universality .[9]

Barroso's global conception (2014) identifies three structuring elements of human dignity: a) Intrinsic value of the person, b) Autonomy of the individual, c) Community value.

The intrinsic value of the human person, in short, corresponds to the nature of the human being and establishes a set of characteristics that are inherent and common to all human beings and that give them a special and superior position in the world, as they are distinct from other species. The author includes in this field the right to life - a basic precondition for the exercise of any other right - as well as the rights to equality before the law, non-discrimination, respect for cultural, linguistic or religious diversity, and the right to physical and psychological integrity (BARROSO, 2014).

There are absolute rights linked to the intrinsic value of the human person, such as the right not to be tortured[10] and the right not to be enslaved[11] , in accordance with the provisions of Articles 7 and 8 of

---

7 "Iaicity assumes that Church and State must be separated, that religion is a private matter for each individual and that, in politics and public affairs, a rational and humanist vision must prevail over religious conceptions." (BARROSO, 2014, p. 73)

8 Neutrality demands that dignity be removed from any particular perfectionist, ideological or political vision, seeking a minimum content of dignity that is accepted by different social and ideological sectors, as well as by those who profess different reasonable conceptions of life. (Ibid.)

9 Universality can be taken from the UDHR (1948) and means that dignity has a universal value, extended to all human beings, respecting multiculturalism. (Ibidem, page 74)

10 See also the Convention against Torture and Other Cruel, Inhuman or Degrading Treatment or Punishment (BRAZIL, 1991).

11 See also the Supplementary Convention on the Abolition of Slavery, the Slave Trade and Institutions and Practices Similar to Slavery (BRAZIL, 1956).

the ICCPR:

Article 7 No one shall be subjected to torture or to cruel, inhuman or degrading treatment or punishment. In particular, it is forbidden to subject a person to a medical or scientific experiment without their free consent.

Article 8 No one shall be subjected to slavery; slavery and the slave trade in all their forms shall be prohibited.

In the area of autonomy, Barroso (2014) teaches that this is the ethical content of human dignity, since it is the foundation of the free will of individuals in the pursuit of social well-being and has self-determination as its central notion. Autonomy corresponds to someone's ability to make decisions and personal choices throughout their life, based on their own conception of the good, without undue extreme influences (Op. Cit., p. 82).

According to this author, autonomy comprises three categories: public autonomy, private autonomy and minimum existential autonomy.

Finally, dignity as a community value emphasizes the role of the state and the community in establishing collective goals and restrictions on individual rights and freedoms in the name of a collective interest, thus representing the social element of dignity. It means relating dignity to the social values of particular communities through weighting and proportionality.

It is important to reaffirm that, together with the right to life, the dignity of the human person irradiates all the other rights currently conceived, whether at international or national level.

In turn, Sarmento (2016) establishes the minimum content of dignity for application at national level, considering four integral elements: a) intrinsic value of the human person; b) autonomy; c) existential minimum and d) recognition.

Sarmento (2016, p. 70) emphasizes the need to delimit the concept of the concrete person, as he considers it vital for defining the contours of the principle of human dignity, and concludes

who is a rational person, but also sentimental and bodily; who is an end in himself and not an "island" separate from society; who must have his autonomy respected, but also needs his basic material needs guaranteed and his identity recognized and respected.

With regard to the first element of dignity, Sarmento (2016) teaches that dignity is used as an intrinsic quality of all human beings, their social *status* or conduct being irrelevant. This means that all individuals who belong to the human species have dignity simply because they are people. This principle prohibits the instrumentalization of the individual for the sake of collective goals or the interests of majorities.

Autonomy, for Sarmento (ibid.), is closely related to the human capacity for self-determination and to positive freedoms. Private autonomy concerns a person's ability to make their own life choices;

public autonomy has a democratic link, empowering all citizens to interfere in the deliberations of the political community.

The existential minimum can be understood as the basic vital guarantees for the exercise of other rights, after all, access to basic material conditions is indispensable for enabling people to exercise their freedom (SEN, 2010).

In Sarmento's (2016) analysis, he states that the existence of material needs that arise from human nature itself, such as access to food, water, housing and health, is unquestionable. However, he warns that the protection of the existential minimum is not limited to guaranteeing physiological human needs, but must go beyond this to include aspects of social life such as access to education, clothing, as well as the protection of a healthy environment. The Brazilian Supreme Court has taken this view:

The existential minimum is not limited to the vital minimum, i.e. the minimum required to live. The content of the existential minimum also includes socio-cultural conditions which, beyond the question of mere survival, ensure that the individual has a minimum level of integration into social life.

Therefore, the existential minimum is a fundamental right directly derived from the principle of human dignity, which manifests itself in both fundamental and social rights, such as health, education, housing, food, social security, social assistance, etc. as well as access to justice. (SARMENTO, 2016)

This has been the position adopted by the Federal Supreme Court in cases involving the content of the existential minimum:

The clause of the reserve of the possible - which cannot be invoked by the public authorities with the aim of defrauding, frustrating or making impossible the implementation of public policies defined in the Constitution itself - finds an insurmountable limitation in the constitutional guarantee of the existential minimum, which represents, in the context of our positive order, a direct emanation of the postulate of the essential dignity of the human person. (...) The notion of 'existential minimum', which results, by implication, from certain constitutional precepts (CF, art. 1, III, and art. 3, III), comprises a complex of prerogatives whose realization is capable of guaranteeing adequate conditions of dignified existence, in order to ensure effective access to the general right to liberty and also to positive services originating from the State, These include the right to education, the right to full protection of children and adolescents, the right to health, the right to social assistance, the right to housing, the right to food and the right to security. Universal Declaration of the Rights of the Human Person, 1948 (Article XXV). " (BRAZIL - STF, 2011)

Finally, the author highlights recognition as the last attribute of dignity and argues that the fulfillment and free development of the human personality are linked to adequate recognition by others. He rightly states that the absence of recognition generates oppression, the establishment of hierarchies and suffering. Non-recognition stems from the devaluation of some identity group, to which negative traits are attributed, which are projected onto all the individuals who make them up, usually due to factors related to ethnicity, sexual orientation, religion, disability, nationality, etc.

In this area of non-recognition, devaluation and stigma, it is important to highlight the intelligence of the concept of vulnerability contained in the document 100 Brasilia Rules on Access to Justice for People in Conditions of Vulnerability (ANADEP, 2008), which attributes subjective elements to the subject, i.e. those inherent to the individual themselves, as well as objective aspects, which are characterized by circumstances capable of generating a state of vulnerability:

(3)	Vulnerable people are those who, because of their age, gender, physical or mental condition, or because of social, economic, ethnic and/or cultural circumstances, find it particularly difficult to fully exercise the rights recognized by the legal system before the justice system.

(4)	The following could be causes of vulnerability, among others: age, disability, belonging to indigenous communities or minorities, victimization, migration and internal displacement, poverty, gender and deprivation of liberty .[12]

It is now understood that situations of vulnerability, alone or in combination, permanently violate one or more categories of human dignity.

Finally, we have tried to establish a minimum content for the protection of the dignity of the human person, seen as the absolute fundamental core of protection and the reason for the existence of the entire system of contemporary human rights.

On the centrality of human dignity, Anderson Schreiber (2013) states precisely:

In Brazil, as in many other countries, human dignity has assumed a prominent position in the legal system. Considered a fundamental principle from which all other principles derive and which guides all legal orders, human dignity has been the guiding value in a process of re-reading the various sectors of law, which are abandoning the liberalism and materialism of yesteryear in favor of recovering another, more humanistic and more supportive approach to legal relations.

2.1.6.2 Individual, Social and Diffuse Rights

When analyzing Brazilian constitutional issues in relation to internationally recognized human rights, Piovesan (2013) considers the 1988 Charter to be a legal milestone in the transition to a democratic regime because it significantly expanded the scope of fundamental rights and guarantees.

The Brazilian Constitution recognizes individual civil and political rights as provided for in the ICCPR (1966), basically in Articles 5 and 14, by stating:

Art. 5 Everyone is equal before the law, without distinction of any kind, and Brazilians and foreigners residing

---

12 See also Mandela Rules - minimum rules for the treatment of prisoners, published by the CNJ in May 2016. Available at
<httn://www.cnj.jus.br/files/conteudo/arquivo/2016/05/39ae8bd2085fdbc4a1b02fa6e3944ba2.ndf>Accessed	on 01/06/16.

in the country are guaranteed the inviolability of the right to life, liberty, equality, security and property, under the following terms:

I - men and women are equal in rights and obligations, under the terms of this Constitution;

(...)

Art. 14: Popular sovereignty shall be exercised through universal suffrage and direct and secret voting, with equal value for all, and, under the terms of the law, through:

I   - plebiscite;

II   - referendum;

III   - popular initiative.

§   1° Voter registration and voting are:

I - compulsory for those over eighteen;

II - optional for:

a)   the illiterate;

b)   those over seventy;

c)   those over sixteen and under eighteen.

(...)

§   3. The following are conditions for eligibility, in accordance with the law:

I   - Brazilian nationality;

II   - the full exercise of political rights;

III   - voter registration;

IV   - electoral domicile in the district;

V   - party affiliation.

In Barroso's (2001) precise exposition, the freedoms provided for in the Brazilian Constitution are concentrated in Article 5 and are set out in its sections:

Freedom of **movement** (*"XV - freedom of movement in the national territory..."*), of **expression** (*"IV - expression of thought; IX - intellectual, artistic, scientific and communication activity; XIV - access to and dissemination of information"*), of **conscience, belief and worship** (*"VI - freedom of conscience and belief is inviolable, and the free exercise of religious cults is ensured..."*), of association (*"XVI - all may peacefully assemble in places open to the public, regardless of authorization...").", freedom of* **assembly** (*"XVI - everyone may assemble peacefully, without arms, in places open to the public, regardless of authorization..."*), freedom of **association** (*"XVII - freedom of association for lawful purposes is full, paramilitary association is* *prohibited"), freedom of* **work** (*"XIII - the exercise of any work, trade or profession is free, subject to the professional qualifications established by law").*

With regard to political rights, provided for in the *aforementioned* Article 14 of the Constitution, Barroso (2001, p. 100) states that these include both nationality rights and citizenship rights:

By the first, the individual is incorporated into the national community for a series of purposes, including prerogatives and duties. By the second, the individual, qualified by certain requirements, is recognized as having electoral capacity (intervention by vote in the composition of state bodies) and elective capacity (personal participation in the composition of state bodies).

In the field of individual law, personality rights are also enshrined as human rights, as can be seen from Art. 17 of the ICCPR (1966)

1.   No one shall be subjected to arbitrary or unlawful interference in his private life, family, home or correspondence, nor to unlawful attacks on his honor and reputation.

2.   Everyone has the right to the protection of the law against such interference or attacks.

Personality rights in Brazil are regulated by the Constitution and the Civil Code of 2002 and consist of essential subjective attributes of the human person, whose legal recognition is the result of a continuous historical journey.

Personality rights are: the right to one's own body - which includes the protection of physical and psychological integrity, the right to one's name, the right to honor, the right to one's image and the right to privacy. (SCHREIBER, 2013)

In the wake of the social rights recognized by the ICESCR (1966), the Charter of the

The 1988 Republic listed them in Articles 6 and 7:

Art. 6 - Social rights are education, health, food, work, housing, transportation, leisure, security, social security, maternity and childhood protection, assistance to the destitute, in the form of this constitution.

Art. 7 - These are the rights of urban and rural workers, as well as others aimed at improving their social condition:

(...)

In order to protect Solidarity or 3rd[a] generation rights, also known as diffuse rights in the Brazilian legal sphere, the 1988 Constitution enshrined the right to a healthy and sustainable environment in Article 225:

Art. 225. Everyone has the right to an ecologically balanced environment, an asset of common use to the people and essential to a healthy quality of life, imposing on the public authorities and the community the duty to defend and preserve it for present and future generations.

Representative democracy, a kind of 4th generation right, was also established by the Constitutional text when it stated in Article 1, § 1 that *"All power emanates from the people, who exercise it through elected representatives or directly, under the terms of this Constitution. "*

In this chapter, the content and characteristics of human rights in the sphere of international law were briefly related to their application in the Brazilian legal system, in order to facilitate an understanding of the normative structure and international protection that exists today in the field of human rights, for their subsequent application as a form of education for citizenship.

2.2 DEVELOPMENT AS FREEDOM

In his famous theory of development as freedom, SEN (2010) seeks to demonstrate how development can be seen as a process of expanding people's real freedoms, not just restricted to the Gross Domestic Product growth index, but taking into account, above all, other determining factors, such as social and economic provisions relating to health and education, for example, and also civil rights linked to effective political participation, which he calls substantive freedoms.

For SEN (2010), the main actor in development is the individual. The author believes that a country's development is closely linked to the opportunities it offers its population to make choices and exercise citizenship. He also states that development can be seen as a process of expanding the real freedoms that people enjoy. He goes on to explain that development must guarantee, independently of economic growth, the social well-being of the community and human rights.

It follows from these statements that, in parallel with the economic growth of a given region or nation, human development must be observed in the same proportion. It's a paradigm shift: with human development, the focus is shifted from economic growth or income to the human being (UNDP, 2016).

The concept of human development was born, defined as a process of expanding people's choices so that they obtain the capacities and opportunities to be what they want to be (UNDP, 2016).

According to the provisions of the Atlas of Human Development[13] , which elucidate the issue very well, this development model must be centered on people and their well-being, to be understood not only as the accumulation of wealth or an increase in income, but mainly as the expansion of the scope of choices and the capacity and freedom to choose. (ATLAS, 2016)

13The Atlas is a platform for consulting the Human Development Index of 5,565 Brazilian municipalities, 27 Federal Units (UF), 20 Metropolitan Regions (RM) and their respective Human Development Units (UDH). The tool provides an overview of human development and internal inequality in municipalities, states and metropolitan regions. Available at <http://www.atlasbrasil.org.br/2013/pt/o atlas/o atlas />Accessed on 01/06/16.

Both human rights and the individual-centered human development model address the guarantee of basic freedoms. Human rights, as explained, express the idea that all people are entitled to social arrangements that protect them from the worst abuses and deprivations, while human development is a process that enhances human capabilities, expands choices and opportunities, so that each person can lead a life of respect and value. It is in this context that human rights and development reinforce each other, expanding people's capacities and protecting their fundamental rights and freedoms (HDR, 2000).

In order to create a counterpoint to another widely used indicator, the Gross Domestic Product (GDP), the Pakistani Mahbub ul Haq with the help of Amartya Sen created the Human Development Index, HDI, as a general and synthetic measure of human development. (UNDP, 2016)

The HDI is made up of three pillars considered fundamental to the expansion of people's freedom: health, education and income.

Health is measured by longevity and translates into the opportunity to lead a long and healthy life. Promoting human development requires ensuring that people live in a healthy environment with access to quality healthcare (UNDP-ATLAS, 2016).

Education, measured by: i) average years of adult education, which is the average number of years of education received over a lifetime by people aged 25 and over; and ii) expected years of schooling for children of school-going age, which is the total number of years of schooling a child of school-going age can expect to receive if prevailing patterns of age-specific enrollment rates remain the same over the child's lifetime; Access to knowledge is a determining and essential factor for well-being and the exercise of individual freedoms, autonomy and self-esteem. "Education builds confidence, confers dignity, broadens horizons and life prospects. " (UNDP-ATLAS, 2016)

Finally, income or standard of living is determined by Gross National Income (GNI) per capita expressed in constant purchasing power parity (PPP), in dollars, with 2005 as the reference year. (UNDP, 2016) Income is a means to a variety of ends and enables the choice of available alternatives and its absence can restrict life opportunities (UNDP-ATLAS, 2016).

According to the Human Development Report[14] carried out in 2000, which adopted Human Rights and Development as its central theme, seven essential aspects are needed for a broader approach to guaranteeing human rights and development:

---

14 The UNDP publishes an annual Global HDR, with cross-cutting themes of international interest, as well as the HDI scale for most of the world's countries. The Human Development Report (HDR) is recognized by the United Nations as an independent intellectual exercise and an important tool for raising awareness of human development around the world. The publication has editorial autonomy guaranteed by a resolution of the United Nations General Assembly. The premise of the first HDR - conceived by the same people who created the HDI - in 1990, was that people are the real wealth of nations, a concept that has guided all subsequent reports. (HDR - UNDP, 2016)

1.   All countries need to strengthen their social arrangements to guarantee human freedoms - with norms, institutions, legal structures and a favorable economic environment. Legislation alone is not enough.

2.   The fulfillment of all human rights requires democracy that is inclusive - protecting the rights of minorities, providing for the separation of powers and ensuring political accountability. Elections alone are not enough.

3.   The eradication of poverty is not just a development objective - it is a central challenge for human rights in the 21st century.

4.   Human rights - in an integrated world - require global justice. The state-centered model of responsibility must be extended to include the obligations of non-state actors and state obligations beyond national borders.

5.   Information and statistics are powerful tools in creating a culture of accountability and realizing human rights. Activists, jurists, statisticians and development experts have to work together with communities. The goal: to generate information and evidence that can break down the barriers of disbelief and mobilize for changes in policy and behaviour.

6.   Achieving full rights for all people in all countries in the 21st century will require action and commitment from key groups in all societies - NGOs, the media and private companies, local and national governments, parliamentary leaders and other opinion leaders.

7.   Human rights and human development cannot be realized universally without stronger international action, in particular to support disadvantaged people and countries and to offset growing global inequalities and marginalization.

In Brazil, the development process has taken on a more humanist character since the National Development and Human Rights Plan - 3, which establishes the guidelines and objectives to be observed when drawing up public policies, as follows:

Guiding Axis II: Development and Human Rights

Guideline 4: Implementing a sustainable development model that is socially and economically inclusive, environmentally balanced and technologically responsible, culturally and regionally diverse, participatory and non-discriminatory.

Strategic objective I: Implementation of public development policies with social inclusion

Strategic objective II: Strengthening family farming and agro-ecological models

Strategic objective III: Promoting research and the implementation of policies for the development of socially inclusive, emancipatory and environmentally sustainable technologies.

Strategic objective IV: Guaranteeing the right to inclusive and sustainable cities.

Guideline 5: Valuing the human person as the central subject of the development process

Strategic Objective I: Ensuring social participation and control in public development policies with a major socio-environmental impact.

Strategic objective II: Affirmation of the principles of human dignity and equity as the foundations of the national development process

Strategic objective III: Strengthening economic rights through public policies for competition and consumer protection

Guideline 6: Promote and protect environmental rights as human rights, including future generations as subjects of rights Strategic Objective I: Affirmation of environmental rights as human rights (PNDH-3, 2010)

As such, there is a marked proximity between the protection of human rights and the development process itself. In this way, human rights education, aimed at the population living in communities in Rio de Janeiro, presents itself as an instrument for realizing development as freedom, as proposed by Sen (2010).

With regard to the socio-economically vulnerable population, Dias (2007) understands that the vicious cycle of poverty and lack of power generates serious, continuous and widespread human rights violations, and in this situation development can help to break this vicious cycle because it aims to alleviate or even eliminate poverty. According to the author, the development of human resources allows for greater participation by traditionally marginalized and excluded sectors of society, which is why it is considered vital in eliminating the structural causes of deprivation, violations and abuses of human rights.

Therefore, Dias (2007) concludes that human rights provide the logical basis, the normative framework and the accountability of those who implement development, given the importance of human rights education for this process that encourages the strengthening and realization of these rights.

2.3 HUMAN RIGHTS EDUCATION

The World Conference on Human Rights considers that education, training and public information on human rights are indispensable for establishing and promoting stable and harmonious relations between communities and for fostering mutual understanding, tolerance and peace" (Vienna Declaration and Program of Action, Part II.D, § 78).

The world's political context with regard to the protection of rights still encounters many obstacles to the recognition of these rights, especially for groups in situations of vulnerability.

Sarmento (2016) recognizes that between the generous discourse of international documents and constitutional texts on human rights, and the concrete lives of the most vulnerable populations, there is a Homeric distance. As the author points out, around the world people continue to be victimized by hunger or easily preventable diseases; human beings are systematically tortured and, when arrested, subjected to absolutely degrading conditions of imprisonment; individuals are discriminated against, humiliated and even murdered because of factors such as ethnicity, nationality, gender, religion, disability or sexual orientation. The dignity of the human person, as proclaimed throughout the human rights protection system, continues to be arbitrarily removed from the daily lives of people, especially the most vulnerable.

Historical facts reinforce the idea of a constant violation of human rights throughout human history. Slavery, the Holy Inquisition, world wars, nuclear bombs, *apartheid* in Africa, the refugee crisis, armed conflicts by extremist groups and terrorism are just a few examples of serious human rights violations that have occurred throughout the history of civilization.

In Brazil's favelas, for example, there is a habitual policy of extermination, selectively targeting poor suspects and residents of these places[15] , which are generally not even investigated (SARMENTO, 2016). There are many examples of populations that, in addition to being marginalized, are also considered disposable, *homo sacer* or killable lives (AGAMBEN, 2007).

The truth is that the world is going through a critical moment and is witnessing the greatest level of human suffering since the Second World War. According to the World Humanitarian Summit[16] , which took place in May 2016 in Istanbul, more than 125 million women, men and children around the world are in need of humanitarian aid due to armed conflicts and disasters (UN - WCH, 2016).

In the best words of Cançado Trindade (2015, p. 21):

"As if the 20th century's sad legacy of tragic contradictions wasn't enough, today, at the dawn of the 21st century, international law is facing new threats to international peace and security, in the midst of a profound crisis that appears to be a real crisis of values on the broadest scale. Never before, as in recent decades, has so much progress in science and technology been tragically accompanied by so much destruction and cruelty. Never before have so many signs of prosperity been alarmingly accompanied by such an increase in economic and social disparities and chronic and extreme poverty. "

The urgency of a new way of conceiving human rights is evident and, to this end, it is essential that their doctrine reaches the greatest number of people. Much is said about human rights, but little is taught, and because of this structural ignorance, completely distorted perceptions of what human rights are arise.

It is therefore crucial to clarify that human rights are now founding principles of modern society,

---

15 Data can be verified in the document "You killed my son" published in 2015 by Amnesty International. Available at <https://anistia.org.br/direitos-humanos/publicacoes/voce-matou-meu- son/>

16The World Humanitarian Summit in Istanbul, May 23-24, aims to mark a major shift in the way the international community prevents human suffering by preparing to respond to crises. For more information, see the document Agenda for Humanity, available at <https://nacoesunidas.org/cupula-mundial-humanitaria-da-onu-propoe-agenda-pela-humanity/>.

since they reflect a culture of protection and respect for others, as well as representing forms of struggle against situations of unequal access to material and immaterial goods, discrimination perpetrated against cultural and religious diversity and, in general, oppression linked to the control of power by minorities. (BRASIL, 2011)

In this sense, it is necessary to conceive a new form of education aimed at building humanist thinking in its essence, based on ideology and behavior. Human rights education essentially sets out to find possible solutions to a serious structural problem in Brazilian culture - ignorance of rights - and to propose a development model based on enhancing the individual's intellectual and behavioral capacities.

The practice of human rights education will encounter various cultural obstacles, which is why the starting point must be the deconstruction of the mistaken conceptualization that has been erected on the terrain of human rights.

2.3.1 Human Rights Education at the International Level

For people to be able to make use of the whole system of human rights protection, everyone - women, men, young people and children - must know and understand the relevance of human rights to their concerns and aspirations. (BENEDEK, 2012)

It means understanding, above all, that the principles and procedures of human rights enable people to participate in decisions that determine their lives, act in conflict resolution and peacekeeping, and constitute a perfectly viable strategy for human, social and economic development centered on the person (BENEDEK, 2012). It should be noted that this centralization is not about radical individualism, but simply about making the individual the protagonist of their own life.

It is from this form of teaching and learning that a culture of human rights will be developed, based on respect, protection, satisfaction, fulfillment and practice of human rights. (Ibidem.)

In this sense, Shulamith Koenig, quoted in the EDH Handbook (BENEDEK, 2012, p. 45), should be highlighted:

Human rights education, learning and dialogue must evoke critical thinking and systemic analysis with a gender perspective on political, civil, economic, social and cultural concerns within the human rights system.

Benedek (2012) suggests that four main objectives should form the basis for human rights education: a) transforming knowledge and information; b) developing skills; c) changing attitudes; and d) taking action.

Item "a" will explain the content, norms and protection related to human rights and what these rights represent in the daily life and work of individuals.

Item "b" means empowering individuals to live and work respecting and implementing human rights, developing skills such as communication, active listening, argumentation and debate, critical analysis, etc.

Changing attitudes consists of reflecting on the relativity of each person's cultural and gender roles in order to rebuild values based on human rights.

Acting in turn aims to implement an awareness of human rights both in everyday life and at work.

Having made these preliminary considerations, we now turn to an analysis of the main international documents on the subject of human rights.

The international community's concern with human rights education was born with the proclamation of the Universal Declaration of Human Rights (1948, p. 14), which included in its text, specifically in item 2 of art. 26 of the document, the following recommendation:

Education shall be directed to the full development of the human personality and to the strengthening of respect for human rights and fundamental freedoms. Education shall promote understanding, tolerance and friendship among all nations and racial or religious groups, and shall support the peace-making activities of the United Nations.

Since then, Cançado Trindade (1993) believes that the declaration has become a pedagogical tool for raising awareness of the fundamental values of democracy and human rights.

Following the 1948 Declaration, Human Rights Education is again recognized in art. 13 of the International Covenant on Economic, Social and Cultural Rights, which was adopted by the XXI Session of the United Nations General Assembly on 19 December 1966 (ICESCR, 1966), which reads as follows:

The States Parties to the present Covenant recognize the _right of everyone to education_. They agree that education shall aim at the _full development of the human personality and of the sense of its dignity and shall strengthen respect for human rights and fundamental freedoms_. They further agree that education should enable all persons to participate effectively in a free society, foster understanding, tolerance and friendship among all nations and among all racial, ethnic or religious groups, and promote the peace-making activities of the United Nations." (emphasis added)

At the Second International Conference on Human Rights, held in 1993 in Vienna, Italy, the reading of Article 33 of the Vienna Declaration shows that the commitment to human rights education is universalized and returns to the agenda of priorities for nations around the world, reiterating the importance of promoting human rights for a culture of respect, tolerance and peace:

33.   The World Conference on Human Rights reaffirms that States are morally obliged, as stipulated in the Universal Declaration of Human Rights, the International Covenant on Economic, Social and Cultural Rights

and other international instruments on human rights, to ensure that education aims to strengthen respect for human rights and fundamental freedoms. The World Conference on Human Rights stresses the importance of including the theme of human rights in education programs and calls on states to do so. Education should promote understanding, tolerance, peace and friendly relations among nations and all racial or religious groups, and encourage the development of United Nations activities in pursuit of these goals. Therefore, human rights education and the dissemination of appropriate information, both theoretical and practical, play an important role in the promotion and respect of human rights for all individuals, without distinction of race, sex, language or religion, which should be included in educational policies at both national and international levels. The World Conference on Human Rights stresses that resource limitations and institutional inadequacies may prevent the immediate realization of these objectives.

Document A/52/469/Supl. 1 of October 20, 1997 (BRAZIL-SDH, 2013) presents a very didactic concept of Human Rights Education:

Human Rights Education can be defined as training, dissemination and information efforts aimed at creating a universal culture of human rights through the transfer of knowledge and skills, as well as the formation of attitudes aimed at: (a) the strengthening of respect for fundamental human rights and freedoms; (b) the full development of the human personality and a sense of dignity; (c) the promotion of understanding, tolerance, gender equality and friendship among all nations, indigenous peoples and racial, national, ethnic, religious and linguistic groups; (d) the possibility for all persons to participate effectively in a free society; (e) the promotion of United Nations peacekeeping activities.

In 1994, the UN General Assembly (UNGA) and the Office of the United Nations High Commissioner for Human Rights (OHCHR) proclaimed the United Nations Decade for Human Rights Education from 1995 to 2004, through Resolution 49/184, and created the International Action Plan for the Decade, which presents in its Article 2 the definition of HRD and then the five main objectives of the project:

34.   In accordance with these provisions, and for the purposes of the Decade, human rights education will be defined as training, dissemination and information efforts aimed at building a universal culture of human rights through the transmission of knowledge and skills and the shaping of attitudes, with a view to:

(a)   Estimating needs and formulating strategies;

(b)   Building and strengthening human rights education programs at the international, regional, national and local levels;

(c)   Development of educational materials;

(d)   Strengthening the role of popular media;

(e)   Global dissemination of the Universal Declaration of Human Rights (OHCHR, 2012, p. 11).

Robinson (apud BENEDEK, 2012) points out that the Decade for Human Rights Education focuses on developing and strengthening comprehensive, effective and sustainable educational programs at international, regional, national and local levels and that national and local initiatives should be encouraged and supported by the international community through the Action Plan presented above, so that states can draw up their own educational guidelines in relation to human rights.

The Plan of Action for the United Nations Decade for Human Rights also established the Guidelines to be followed by States in drawing up National Action Plans (UN-UNHCHR, 1994), which will focus on:

(a)   Establish or strengthen national and local human rights institutions and organizations;

(b)   Take steps to introduce national programs for the promotion and protection of human rights, as recommended by the World Conference on Human Rights;

(c)   Prevent human rights violations that result in ruinous human, social, cultural, environmental and economic costs;

(d)   Identify those members of society who are currently deprived of the full enjoyment of human rights and ensure that effective measures are taken to remedy this situation;

(e)   Enabling a comprehensive response to rapid social and economic changes that could otherwise result in chaos and instability;

(f)   Promote the diversity of sources, approaches, methodologies and institutions in the field of human rights education;

(g)   Increase opportunities for cooperation in human rights education activities between public services, non-governmental organizations, professional groups and other civil society institutions;

(h)   Emphasize the role of human rights in national development;

(i)   To help governments fulfill the commitments they have previously made regarding human rights education under international instruments and programs, in particular the Vienna Declaration and Program of Action (1993) and the United Nations Decade for Human Rights Education (1995-2004).

This document reinforces the idea of the essentiality of human rights education for the reduction of human rights violations and for the construction of free, just and peaceful societies.

In this context, on December 10, 2004, the UNGA proclaimed a new World Program for EDH through Resolution 59/113-A, which was to be implemented through action plans every 3 years. The action plan for the first phase[17] (2005-2009) of the World Program for EDH focuses on primary and secondary school systems. The action plan for the second phase focuses on higher education in human

---

17full document available at
<http://www.dhnet.org.br/dados/textos/edh/br/plano action world program edh en.pdf> Accessed on 01/06/16.

rights training programs for teachers and educators, civil servants, police officers and the military[18] (2010-2015). The third phase[19] (2015-2019), currently in force, is dedicated to reinforcing the implementation of the first two phases and promoting human rights training for professionals committed to information as well as journalists, bloggers and media professionals.

The Action Plans contain measures that the Ministries of Education and other actors in the education system and civil society should jointly adopt to integrate human rights education into all educational levels and specific professional systems.

According to UNESCO (2006), human rights education can be defined as:

a set of education, training and information dissemination activities aimed at creating a universal culture of human rights. Comprehensive human rights education not only provides knowledge about human rights and the mechanisms to protect them, but also imparts the skills needed to promote, defend and apply human rights in people's daily lives. Human rights education promotes the attitudes and behavior necessary for human rights for all members of society to be respected.

Provisions on human rights have been incorporated into numerous international documents, in particular the Universal Declaration of Human Rights (Article 26), the International Covenant on Economic, Social and Cultural Rights (Article 13), the Convention on the Rights of the Child (Article 29), the Convention on the Elimination of All Forms of Discrimination against Women (Article 10), the International Convention on the Elimination of All Forms of Racial Discrimination (article 7) and the Vienna Declaration and Program of Action (Part I, paragraphs 33 and 34 and Part II, paragraphs 78 to 82), as well as in the Declaration and Program of Action of the World Conference Against Racism, Racial Discrimination, Xenophobia and Related Intolerance, held in Durban (South Africa) in 2001 (Declaration, paragraphs 95 to 97 and Program of Action, paragraphs 129 to 139). (UNESCO, 2006)

Still in the context of the Action Plan for the first phase, PMEDH-1 (UNESCO, 2006), it is possible to find a clear definition of human rights education as the set of training and information dissemination activities aimed at creating a universal culture in the sphere of human rights through the transmission of knowledge, the teaching of techniques and the formation of attitudes, and it also establishes its main objectives:

a)   Strengthen respect for human rights and fundamental freedoms;

b)   To fully develop the human personality and the sense of human dignity;

c)   To promote understanding, tolerance, gender equality and friendship among all nations, indigenous

---

18 full document available at <httn://unesdoc.unesco.org/images/0021/002173/217350nor.ndf>Accessed on 01/06/2016.
19full document available at <http://unesdoc.unesco.org/images/0023/002329/232922PQR.ndf>
Accessed on 01/06/16.

peoples and racial, national, ethnic, religious and linguistic groups;

d)   To facilitate the effective participation of all people in a free and democratic society in which the rule of law prevails;

e)   Fostering and maintaining peace;

f)   Promote sustainable development centered on people and social justice (UNESCO, 2006, p. 10).

It is also worth highlighting the three main dimensions of human rights education presented by UNESCO (2006, p. 10)

a)   Knowledge and skills: learning about human rights and the mechanisms for their protection, as well as acquiring the ability to apply them in everyday life;

b)   Values, attitudes and behaviors: promoting values and strengthening attitudes and behaviors that respect human rights;

c)   Adoption of measures: encourage the adoption of measures to defend and promote human rights.

In this way, the Action Plan establishes a series of objectives and methods for implementing policies that make human rights education more effective and stronger as an instrument of social awareness and transformation.

On December 19, 2011, the UNGA adopted the United Nations Declaration on Human Rights Education and Training through Resolution 66/173 and requested that governments, United Nations bodies and organizations, intergovernmental organizations and NGOs intensify their efforts to disseminate the declaration and promote its respect and understanding at a universal level.

It is worth noting that the Declaration reaffirms the understanding that everyone has the right to education, and that education should be guided by the full development of the human personality and its dignity, enabling all persons to participate effectively in a free society, fostering understanding, tolerance and friendship among all nations and all racial, ethnic and religious groups, and promoting the development of the activities of the United Nations for the maintenance of peace, security and the strengthening of human rights.

Article 1 of the Declaration considers the right to seek and receive information on all human rights to be a universal human right, and to this end access to human rights education and training must be guaranteed. (UN, 2012)

This was a brief overview of the main international documents dealing with human rights education, and many of the declarations currently in force in international law deal with the humanist formation of human beings.

2.3.2 Human Rights Education in Brazil

From a legal-normative point of view, education in Brazil has the constitutional status of a social right, one of the categories included in Title II of the 1988 Federal Constitution, which deals with the fundamental rights and guarantees inherent to all individuals, as established in Article 6:

Social rights are education, health, food, work, housing, transportation, leisure, security, social security, maternity and childhood protection, assistance to the destitute, in the form of this Constitution. (BRASIL, 1988)

The objectives of education in Brazil can be found in Article 205 of the Brazilian Constitution, which reads as follows:

Education, the right of all and the duty of the State and the family, will be promoted and encouraged with the collaboration of society, aiming at the full development of the person, their preparation for the exercise of citizenship and their qualification for work (BRASIL, 1988).

It is safe to say that education represents, in its broad sense, everything that can be done to develop the human being, and, in the strict sense, instruction and the improvement of skills and abilities. (VIANNA, 2006)

For Freire (1967), the starting point for education is to consider freedom and criticism as the individual's way of being. In a society divided into classes, education is a powerful tool for social change. Freire (op. Cit.) also argues that education for development must be a practice of permanent awareness-raising, enabling people to courageously discuss their problems and, from this, gain the strength and courage needed to fight and become the protagonists of their own lives. A true pedagogy of the oppressed: one that has to be forged with the human being and not for him, in the incessant struggle to recover his humanity. (FREIRE, 2014).

Article 214 of the 1988 Constitution states that the law must establish a National Education Plan, lasting ten years, with the aim of articulating the national education system and defining guidelines, objectives, targets and implementation strategies to ensure the maintenance and development of education at its various levels, highlighting in item V the sovereign concern with the humanistic promotion of the country, including education in human rights.

The National Education Plan, which has a ten-year duration (2014-2024), was approved by Law 13.005 of June 25, 2014 to regulate Article 214 and adopts in its text clear provisions on human rights education. Among the guidelines set out in Article 2, it is worth highlighting:

V - training for work and citizenship, with an emphasis on the moral and ethical values on which society is based;

VII - humanistic, scientific, cultural and technological promotion of the country; X - promotion of the principles of respect for human rights, diversity and socio-environmental sustainability.

The Law of Guidelines and Bases (BRASIL, 1996) states in Article 1 that education:

encompasses the formative processes that develop in family life, in human coexistence, at work, in educational and research institutions, in social movements and civil society organizations, and in cultural manifestations.

Among the principles listed in Article 3 of the School Education Guidelines and Bases Law (1996), it is possible to see that some are based on aspects of humanist education, namely:

Teaching will be based on the following principles:

I - freedom to learn, teach, research and disseminate culture, thought, art and knowledge;

III   - pluralism of ideas and pedagogical concepts;

IV   - respect for freedom and appreciation of tolerance; XII - consideration of ethnic-racial diversity.

Human rights education in Brazil has taken on a more expressive form since the 1980s, based on the country's re-democratization movement (PNEDH, 2007), which put an end to a dictatorial regime marked by state authoritarianism and violations of individual rights and guarantees. This movement reached its legal milestone with the promulgation of the Federal Constitution in 1988 (BRASIL, 1998), which legitimately enshrined the Democratic Rule of Law and recognized as its foundations respect for the dignity of the human person and the guarantee of individual and collective rights, such as civil and political rights and economic, social, cultural and environmental rights.

Rights-based education proposes that in addition to the basic subjects taught in educational environments, human rights education should be included as a useful tool for strengthening a culture of rights in which human rights values prevail.

In this sense, in order to recognize and realize education as a human right of a social nature and Human Rights Education as one of the fundamental axes of the right to education, society will need to demonstrate a firm stance on promoting a culture of rights. (BRASIL, 2011)

Specifically, human rights education aims to raise awareness, transform and emancipate contemporary society through knowledge and, as Benevides (2000) teaches, it is essentially about forming a culture of respect for the dignity of the human person through the promotion and defense of fundamental values such as life, freedom, equality, justice, solidarity, cooperation, tolerance and peace.

Indeed, Benevides (2009, p. 323) teaches that Education in Rights

Humans start from three main points:

Human Rights Education starts from three essential points: firstly, it is an education of a permanent, continuous and global nature. Secondly, it is an education necessarily geared towards change and thirdly, it is an inculcation of values, to reach hearts and minds and not just instruction, merely the transmission of knowledge.

Furthermore, and no less importantly, either this education is shared by those involved in the educational process - educators and students - or it is not human rights education. These points are premises: continuing education, education for change and comprehensive education, in the sense of being shared and reaching both reason and emotion.

Based on this explanation, it is possible to identify three main axes of HRD: i) educating for principles; ii) educating for values; iii) educating for rights.

It is also possible to identify a fourth axis of the EHR, which consists of education for deconstruction, insofar as the EHR aims to deconstruct discriminatory ideas and attitudes of prejudice against certain historically vulnerable groups, reiterating the equality of human beings in dignity and rights.

It is in this historical context that the first versions of the National Program of

Human Rights (PNDH), produced between 1996 and 2002. With regard to the theme of Human Rights Education, the main guiding document is the National Human Rights Program-3, known as PNDH-3 (2009), which, in its guiding axis V, sets out the determinations on Human Rights Education and Culture with a focus on developing a new collective mentality for exercising solidarity, respect for diversity and tolerance, as well as combating prejudice, discrimination and violence, promoting the adoption of new values of freedom, justice and equality.

With regard to non-formal education, there is a specific provision in Guideline No. 20 of Guiding Axis V, Strategic Objective I of the PNDH-3 (2009), Programmatic Action I, item "b", which deals with the inclusion of the theme of human rights education in non-formal education, which is the responsibility of the Special Secretariat for Human Rights of the Presidency of the Republic, the Ministry of Culture, the Special Secretariat for Policies to Promote Racial Equality of the Presidency of the Republic; the Special Secretariat for Human Rights of the Presidency of the Republic; the Special Secretariat for Human Rights of the Presidency of the Republic; and the Special Secretariat for Human Rights of the Ministry of Culture.

Policies for Women of the Presidency of the Republic; Ministry of Justice in order to:

b) To support popular human rights education initiatives developed by community organizations, social movements, non-governmental organizations and other organized agents of civil society.

In 2006, Brazil conceived its first National Plan for Human Rights Education, drawn up by the Special Secretariat for Human Rights of the Presidency of the Republic in partnership with executive branch bodies, specifically the Ministries of Education and Justice, and with the collaboration of UNESCO, to establish an educational policy for the Brazilian state aimed at the five main educational spheres (MEC, 2011): basic education, higher education, non-formal education, the media and the training of public security and justice agents.

The National Plans are implemented by public policies to be developed by the municipalities in collaboration with the other spheres of public power. The National Human Rights Education Plan incorporates the main aspects of international human rights documents, taking into account society's ancient and contemporary demands for the construction of a culture of peace, democracy, development and social justice. (PORTAL BRASIL, 2011)

According to the National Plan for Human Rights Education (2007), non-formal human rights education is guided by the principles of emancipation and autonomy, with the aim of carrying out the process of raising awareness and building a critical conscience, and can be understood as education for life in the sense of guaranteeing respect for the dignity of the human being.

Human Rights Education, as advocated by the PNEDH (2007), is seen as a multidimensional and systematic process that leads to the formation of the subject of rights, made up of 5 guiding dimensions:

a)   apprehension of historically constructed knowledge about human rights and their relationship with international, national and local contexts;

b)   affirmation of values, attitudes and social practices that express the culture of human rights in all areas of society;

c)   the formation of a citizen's conscience capable of being present at the cognitive, social, ethical and political levels;

d)   development of participatory methodological processes and collective construction, using contextualized didactic languages and materials;

e)   strengthening individual and social practices that generate actions and instruments for the promotion, protection and defense of human rights, as well as the reparation of violations.

The PNEDH is the main national document guiding public policies and civil society actions for human rights education at national level, and points out the objectives to be achieved in the implementation of the Plan (2007):

a)   highlight the strategic role of human rights education in strengthening the democratic rule of law;

b)   emphasize the role of human rights in building a just, equitable and democratic society;

c)   encourage the development of human rights education actions by public authorities and civil society through joint actions;

d)   contribute to the implementation of international and national commitments to human rights education;

e)   stimulate national and international cooperation in the implementation of human rights education actions;

f)   propose that human rights education be mainstreamed in public policies, stimulating the institutional and inter-institutional development of the actions provided for in the PNEDH in the most diverse sectors (education, health, communication, culture, security and justice, sport and leisure, among others);

g)   making progress on the actions and proposals of the National Human Rights Program (PNDH) with regard to human rights education issues;

h)   to guide educational policies aimed at creating a culture of human rights;

i)   establish objectives, guidelines and lines of action for the development of programs and projects in the area of human rights education;

j)   to encourage reflection, study and research into human rights education;

k)   encourage the creation and strengthening of national, state and municipal institutions and organizations in the field of human rights education;

l)   to guide the drafting, implementation, monitoring, evaluation and updating of the Human Rights Education Plans of the states and municipalities;

m)   encourage access to human rights education for people with disabilities.

According to item "L" above, the Plan delegates the drafting, implementation, monitoring, evaluation and updating of local Human Rights Education Plans to the states and municipalities, which must create and implement these provisions:

The PNEDH (2007) also establishes the guiding principles of non-formal human rights education, as follows :[20]

a)   qualification for work;

b)   adoption and community-oriented practices;

c)   political learning of rights through participation in social groups;

d)   education in the media;

e)   learning formal schooling content in different modalities; and

f)   education for life in order to guarantee respect for the dignity of the human being.

For its part, the 1st Municipal Human Rights Plan for Rio de Janeiro (2014) reaffirms that education and culture in human rights aim to form a new collective concept for the exercise of solidarity, respect for diversity and tolerance, with the main objectives of combating prejudice, discrimination and violence, as well as promoting values such as equality, justice and freedom, and enshrines the

---

20 Full original text: "Non-formal human rights education is guided by the principles of emancipation and autonomy. Its implementation is a permanent process of sensitization and formation of critical awareness, directed towards the forwarding of demands and the formulation of proposals for public policies, and can be understood as:" (PNEDH, 2007, p. 42)

expression "Rio de direitos. "

The document assigns responsibility for the policy of education and culture in human rights to Guiding Axis V, and specifically to Guideline No. 3, responsibility for recognizing non-formal education as a space for the defense and promotion of human rights.

The species to be explored and used in this work is solely non-formal education. As Gohn (2006) explains, this form of education is that which takes place through the evolution and experiences of human life itself, via processes of sharing experiences, and can be exercised in collective and everyday spaces and actions, as well as in public spaces.

For the author (GOHN, 2006, p. 29), non-formal education not only enables individuals to become citizens of the world in the world, but also broadens the horizons of knowledge about the individuals of the world and their forms of sociability, prioritizing both the construction of social relationships based on equality and social justice and the transmission of information and political and socio-cultural training, as both are capable of strengthening the exercise of citizenship.

In 2012, the National Education Council established the National Guidelines for Human Rights Education through Resolution No. 01/2012, taking into account the provisions of international and national documents[21] on the subject.

It is worth highlighting the principles on which education for social change and transformation will be based, according to Resolution No. 01/2012:

I   - human dignity;

II   - equal rights;

III   - recognizing and valuing differences and diversity;

IV   - secularity of the state;

V   - democracy in education;

VI   - transversality, experience and globality; and

VII   - socio-environmental sustainability.

In the wake of national documents on human rights education, it is important to highlight the inclusion

---

21 It is important to transcribe the full text to demonstrate the breadth of this work's approach to the main documents on humanist education "CONSIDERING the provisions of the Universal Declaration of Human Rights of 1948; the United Nations Declaration on Human Rights Education and Training (Resolution A/66/137/2011); the Federal Constitution of 1988; the Law of Guidelines and Bases of National Education (Law no. 9.394/1996); the World Program for Human Rights Education (PMEDH 2005/2014), the National Human Rights Program (PNDH-3/Decree No. 7.037/2009); the National Plan for Human Rights Education (PNEDH/2006); and the national guidelines issued by the National Education Council, as well as other national and international documents aimed at ensuring the right to education for all." (CNE, 2012)

of humanist education values in the training of teaching professionals in basic education through the promulgation of the National Curriculum Guidelines for Bachelor's Degrees, defined by Resolution No. 02/2015 of the National Education Council, a body linked to the Ministry of Education, both of the Executive Branch. Even in the preamble, the concern with the matter is evident, given that the Resolution considers education in and for human rights to be a fundamental right and an integral part of the right to education, as well as

a means of putting into effect all the human rights recognized by the Brazilian state in its legal system and by the countries that are fighting to strengthen democracy, and that human rights education is a strategic necessity in the training of teaching professionals and in educational action in line with the National Guidelines for Human Rights Education;

This resolution innovates and elevates to the status of a principle premises deriving from human rights education, by establishing in art. 2, §5, II:

§ Paragraph 5 are the principles of the Training of Basic Education Teaching Professionals:

II - the training of teaching professionals (trainers and students) as a commitment to a social, political and ethical project that contributes to the consolidation of a sovereign, democratic, just, inclusive nation that promotes the emancipation of individuals and social groups, attentive to the recognition and appreciation of diversity and therefore opposed to all forms of discrimination.

The implementation of human rights education in the training of teaching professionals reinforces the expansion of the policy of protection and promotion of human rights and can be considered an inaugural stage for an educational and cultural transformation based on humanist values.

As Coutinho (2013) rightly points out, access to education is a factor clearly related to inequality, since people who have access to education are, as a rule, those who will appropriate more significant portions of wealth, while those who have not had full access to education and do not benefit from any redistributive policy, tend to be left with reduced portions of income and therefore pass on this underprivileged situation to their descendants, generating a vicious cycle of elite reproduction and reduced social mobility.

Nonetheless, human rights education aims to guarantee students an impartial education, free of preconceived values, based on respect, solidarity and otherness, which unveils reality and provides theoretical, historical, social and legal support for students to develop their own critical thinking. By reinforcing critical thinking, a filter is created for the reception of absolute truths without question and a prosperous path is opened for ideas based on facts and not on any form of mythology. EDH aims to instill values of respect, tolerance, otherness, solidarity, social justice and to stabilize a culture of peace in everyday practices.

More than ever, the world needs Human Rights Education, to recognize that we are all human, equal in dignity and rights.

2.4 Casa do Trabalhador - Manguinhos Community

This research was carried out inside the Casa do Trabalhador, in the Manguinhos community, during the execution of the Manguinhos Project - a free legal assistance and guidance program for the population, developed by the researcher through the Augusto Motta University Center. The program took place on Tuesdays from 9:00 to 12:00.

Manguinhos [22][23] is a community in Rio de Janeiro, located between Benfica and Bonsucesso. Of Rio's 128 neighborhoods, Manguinhos occupies the 5^a worst position in the HDI ranking by neighborhood (IBGE, 2000), demonstrating that in this community, education, health and income are precarious.

As Coutinho (2013) rightly points out, the greater the inequality, the higher the index of social and health problems, but conversely, the lower the levels of inequality, the lower the incidence of health problems, violence, depression, among others. The author states that, in general, factors linked to work and the unequal appropriation of its income, the distribution of rural and urban property, education, issues of race, gender, culture, as well as historical patterns of development in each society are referred to as present, past and potentially future sources of inequality.

In Rio de Janeiro, the term community or favela is traditionally used. Unfortunately, the terms favela and favelado represent categories of accusation, which stigmatize the social dimension of geography and project prejudices onto an entire population (SOARES, 2014).

The government's official definition of the term favela reflects an inexorable unhappiness, with the use of long-winded, pejorative and strongly value-laden definitions (Op. Cit.) which, at this point, must be transcribed:

This is a complex made up of 51 or more housing units characterized by the absence of title deeds and at least one of the following characteristics: - irregular circulation routes and the size and shape of plots and/or - lack of essential public services (such as garbage collection, sewage system, water system, electricity and public lighting). (IBGE, 2010)

It doesn't take a detailed analysis to realize that the state considers the favela to be a place of permanent vulnerability, a situation that makes access to human rights much more complex than for the rest of the population, which is why targeting these inhabitants is an unquestionably necessary measure, especially considering the results obtained.

The aim is to foster a sense of citizen participation among these people, placing individuals at the

---

22 History of Manguinhos. Available at <http://www.conhecendomanguinhos.fiocruz.br/?q=node/15>
23 See also Rio+Social - Manguinhos. Available at <http://www.riomaissocial.org/territorios/manguinhos/>

center and target of development, in a circle of empowerment and emancipation.

There is no longer any room for the naturalization of discriminatory practices against economically vulnerable groups, after all, how can a person who survives amidst the most varied forms of deprivation and suffering be socially condemned, precisely because they haven't had opportunities?

The strengthening of spaces of multiple vulnerabilities can be fostered through HRD, which, from its very content, rises up against the naturalization of inequalities and proposes to formulate a critical sense for the individual to understand himself in the world and become able to influence the development process.

As Soares (2014, p. 2) brilliantly stated, "There will no longer be the quiet that comes from the peace of cemeteries and the naturalization of inequalities, stigmas and racism." (SOARES, 2014, p. 12)

3 METHODOLOGY

3.1 Research delimitation

This research, structured as Action Research, aims to implement a non-formal human rights education program in a socio-economically vulnerable community located in the North Zone of the city of Rio de Janeiro, precisely in the Complexo de Manguinhos.

The purpose of this study was to investigate whether the human rights knowledge of the group studied was sufficient for them to exercise citizenship and, if not, whether they were interested in building new knowledge.

The research was based on the following hypothesis: the research group's knowledge of human rights is insufficient to exercise citizenship.

When dealing with non-formal education, the PNEDH states that the process of education, reflection and learning takes place permanently, and is not limited to school environments, but extends to homes, workplaces, social organizations, etc.

Action Research allows the researcher to intervene directly in a social problem, analyzing it and announcing its objective in such a way as to mobilize the participants in the construction of new knowledge, and specifically in the present case, with regard to knowledge in human rights.

The final product will be a non-formal human rights education program based on the data collected on the group surveyed.

The methodology will be qualitative, based on the results obtained.

3.2 Research stages

1ª Stage: Analysis of the subject matter

Stage 2: Literature review

Stage 3: Application of the survey instrument to the study group

Stage 4: Evaluation of results

Stage 5: Preparation of a special program for human rights education in Manguinhos/RJ in the non-formal mode

3.3 *Locus* of Research

The practical development of the research was carried out inside the Casa do Trabalhador in Manguinhos, comprising the group of users who seek legal assistance offered by UNISUAM through the Manguinhos Project - Free Legal Assistance and Guidance Program in Manguinhos, aged between

18 and 65, between the months of September and December 2015.

3.4 Research Instrument

The evaluation of the work carried out with the group studied was based on a closed questionnaire with 4 specific questions about knowledge of human rights.

Data was also collected on social issues such as housing, work, health and leisure, health and the environment and social assistance, with the aim of observing the main deficiencies in relation to social rights in order to help develop human rights education content based on the results obtained.

4 RESULTS AND DISCUSSION

Group surveyed: 23 interviewees, men and women aged between 18 and 65, residents of the Manguinhos community, who sought legal assistance at the Manguinhos Project - UNISUAM, from September 2015 to December 2015, on Tuesdays from 9:00 to 12:00.

3.5 Group of Questions 1:

The specific questions on the human rights knowledge base were about:

1) Prior cognition in human rights;

2) Interest in learning about human rights;

3) Knowledge of the main human rights protection bodies;

4) Interest in participating in an EDH course;

Table 1 Specific questions on human rights

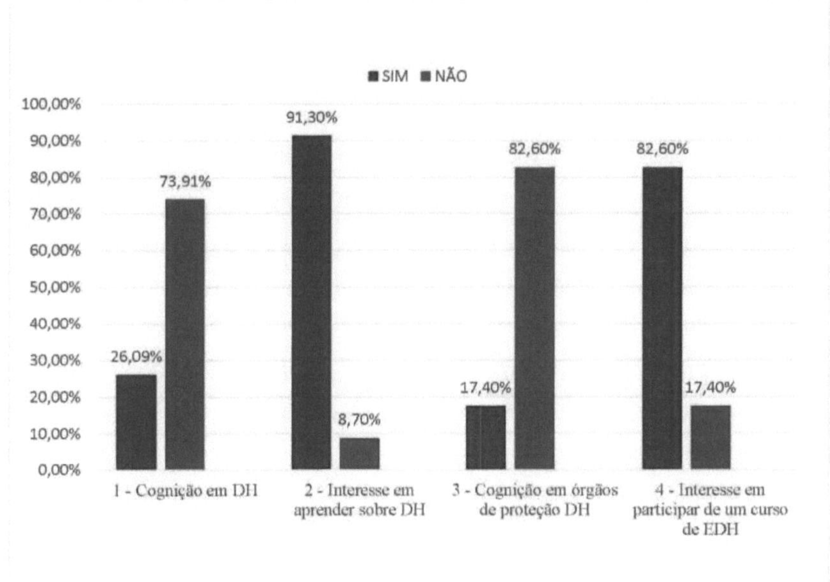

The first group of the survey instrument to be analyzed consists of specific questions about human rights (1) and their protection mechanisms (3) as well as the group's interest in acquiring knowledge about the subject (2) and about participating in a human rights education course (4).

The result shown in item 1 of the graph reveals that 73.91% of the people interviewed answered negatively to the question about whether they had previous knowledge of human rights, a fact that reinforces the hypothesis put forward in the study about the insufficiency of human rights knowledge for exercising citizenship.

For people to be able to freely dispose of and protect their rights, they first need to know about them. It is only through legal education with an emphasis on human rights that the process of development as freedom proposed by SEN (2010) will become viable. In this case, access to human rights education is a fundamental right to be promoted and protected, both by the state and by civil society, especially as it is aimed at groups in situations of vulnerability, as is the case in Rio de Janeiro's communities.

In this sense, Candau () teaches that human rights education has three main objectives: to form subjects of rights, to promote processes of empowerment and to educate for social transformation. It is worth remembering that education is one of the pillars of the HDI.

Therefore, the National Plan for Human Rights Education (2007) enshrined as its guiding dimension the strengthening of individual and social practices that generate actions and instruments in favor of the promotion, protection and defense of human rights, as well as the reparation of violations. The first step is to learn about the rights protected by the legal system.

In the same vein, Dias (2014) asserts that human rights provide the logical basis, normative framework and responsibility for those implementing development, given the importance of human rights education for this process, which encourages the strengthening and realization of rights.

For people to be able to make use of the whole system of human rights protection, everyone needs to know and understand the relevance of human rights to their concerns and aspirations. (BENEDEK, 2012)

It means understanding, above all, that human rights principles and procedures enable people to participate in decisions that determine their lives, act in conflict resolution and peacekeeping, and constitute a perfectly viable strategy for human, social and economic development centered on the person (BENEDEK, 2012).

The result shown in item 2 of the graph shows that 91.30% of the people interviewed responded positively about having an interest in learning about human rights. This is a very optimistic result, given the urgent need to produce human rights education in today's world.

Item 3 shows a high level of ignorance about human rights protection bodies, with 82.60% of those interviewed answering the question in the negative. This data reveals a greater difficulty for this group in seeking legal protection in the event of a possible violation. Lack of knowledge about protection mechanisms is a real obstacle to people fully exercising the rights recognized by the legal system before the judicial system. Information on human rights protection at national and international level will be included in the final product of this research.

Finally, 82.60% of those interviewed said they were interested in taking a human rights course, demonstrating the need to implement education in this form, with humanist training aimed at social transformation.

3.6 GROUP OF QUESTIONS 2

The second group of questions sought to verify some of the group's social data, in order to help prepare the content of the Special Human Rights Education Program, presented as the final product of this research.

Table 2 Social information on income

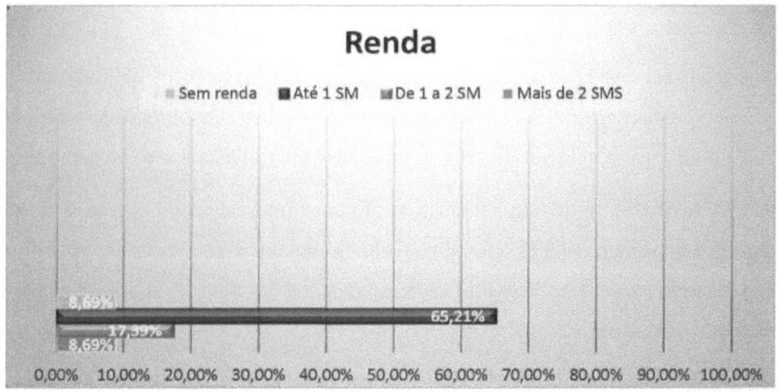

Graph 2 shows that 65.21% of the people interviewed have an income of up to one minimum wage, 17.39% have an income of between one and two minimum wages and 8.69% have an income of more than two minimum wages and the same proportion do not have any kind of fixed income. There is therefore a clear condition of economic vulnerability affecting a significant majority of the group surveyed, which is why the need to include content on public income policies is evident, for example PRONATEC, the National Employment System, welfare benefits and plans to encourage individual micro-entrepreneurs.

Table 3 Education

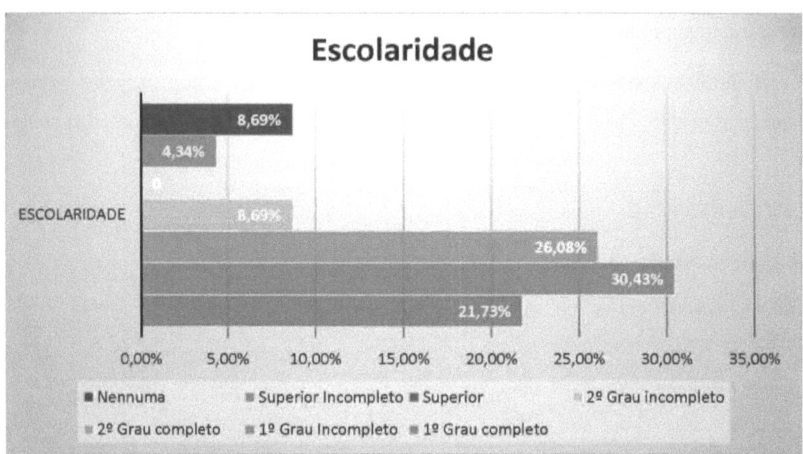

Graph 3 shows that the group surveyed had a low level of schooling, with the majority of interviewees having incomplete primary education (30.43%). These results show that low schooling and precarious access to education are conditions of vulnerability that compromise the full exercise of human rights.

This scenario is perfectly favorable to the implementation of non-formal education, given that this modality does not require a minimum level of schooling. Gohn () explains that non-formal education enables individuals to become citizens of the world as it expands the horizons of knowledge about individuals and their social relationships.

As precisely pointed out by Coutinho (2013), access to education is a factor clearly related to inequality since people who have access to education are, as a rule, those who will appropriate more significant portions of wealth and those who have not had full access to education and do not benefit from any redistributive policy, tend to be left with reduced portions of income and therefore pass on this underprivileged situation to their descendants, generating a vicious cycle of elite reproduction and reduced social mobility.

In this context, a model of non-formal education that is provided in a simple, didactic and objective way becomes important, in view of the deficits revealed in the research.

Table 4 Work

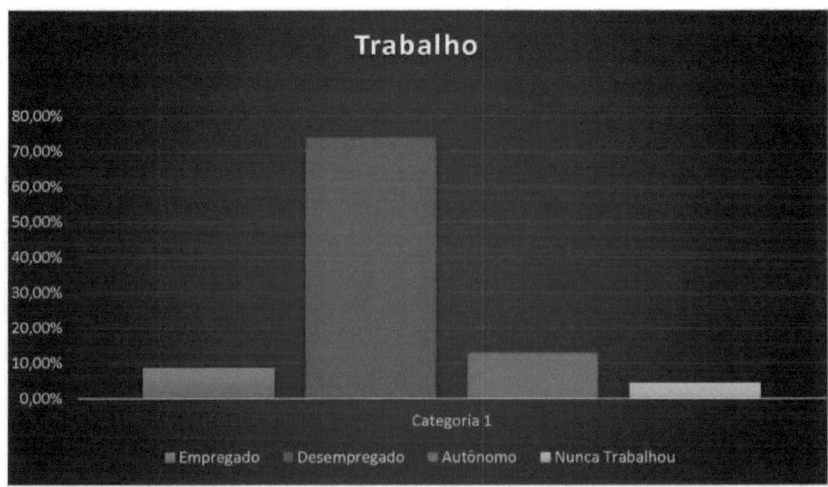

Table 4 shows a high unemployment rate of 73.91% among the group surveyed. With regard to work, the content of the EDH course should include provisions relating to the CLT and labor rights such as severance pay, working hours, overtime, bonuses, the possibility of termination for just cause by the employee and employer, among others, strengthening knowledge of a primary issue directly linked to human subsistence in a capitalist model of production, the right to work.

Table 5 Environment and Social Assistance

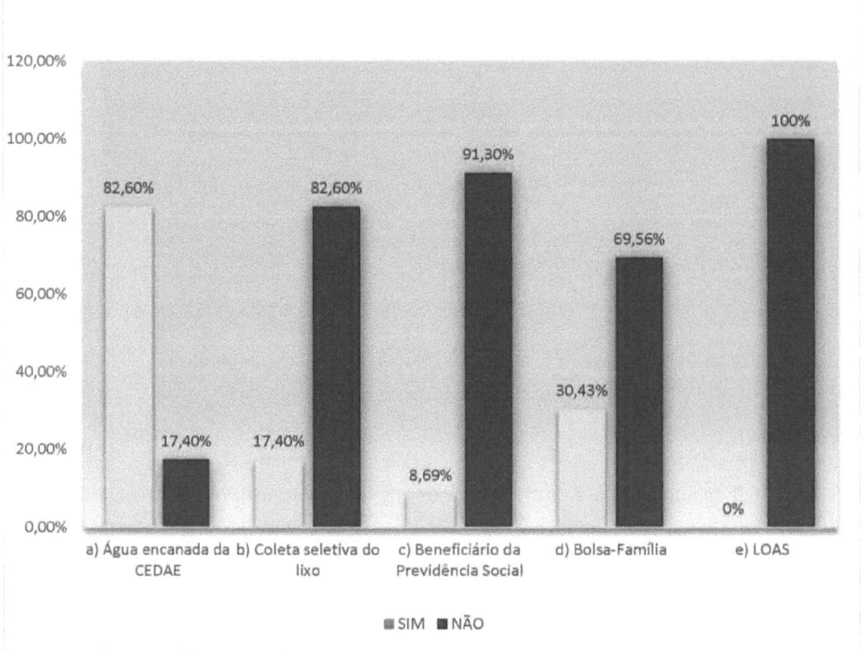

Table 5 analyzes data on the environment and assistance, both of which are part of the normative system of human rights, assistance being a human right of a social nature, while the environment is a human right of a diffuse nature.

Item a showed that 82.60% of the interviewees responded positively to the question about the availability of piped water in their homes. This data points to progress on the issue of the right to the city in terms of access to urban resources. The right to the city will also be addressed in the content of the program.

In the opposite direction was the analysis of selective waste collection in item b, in which 82.60% of respondents answered in the negative, representing a lack of access to selective waste collection. This data points to the need for theoretical and behavioral reinforcement of the right to the environment. Selective waste collection is an important policy for sustainable development, directly linked to the right to a healthy environment, a topic that will be included in the final product.

Item C found that 91.3% of those interviewed were not social security beneficiaries, while 8.69% answered that they received some kind of benefit. Social security is a human right of a social nature which aims to guarantee the income of the contributor or their dependents when one of the so-called social risks occurs: old age, illness, disability, death, deprivation of liberty. There is a clear need to

48

broaden knowledge about the institute itself, its benefits and the requirements to be a beneficiary, content that should be included in the EDH Program.

Bolsa Familia is a direct cash transfer program aimed at families living in poverty and extreme poverty in Brazil, so that they can overcome the condition of vulnerability resulting from socio-economic disadvantage.

The objectives of the PBF are: to combat hunger by encouraging food and nutritional security, to promote access for the poorest families to the network of public services (health, education and social assistance), to support the development of families living in poverty and extreme poverty, to combat poverty and inequality and to encourage public authorities in all their spheres to operate in conjunction with relevant social policies (COUTINHO, 2013).

According to data from the Ministry of Social Development[24] , approximately 36 million Brazilians would be in extreme poverty today if the PBF didn't exist. We need to disseminate this statistical data through EDH so that people know and recognize the magnitude of this social program, which is almost always questioned precisely because of its lack of knowledge.

The inclusion of conditionalities in the acquisition of the PBF benefit in the final product of the survey is also relevant, given that 30.43% of the group interviewed said they were beneficiaries of the program. It is worth remembering that all families with a monthly income per person of up to R$ 77.00 or families with a *per capita* income of between R$ 77.01 and R$ 154.00 are entitled to receive the PBF, as long as they include children or adolescents aged 0 to 17.[25]

Last but not least, item E asks about the receipt of the Beneficio da Prestaçao Continuada, commonly known as BPC- LOAS because it was established in the Organic Law on Social Assistance, in its article 20.

However, from a reading of art. 20, *caput* and §3 of LOAS, two considerations need to be highlighted:

Art. 20: The continued benefit is a guarantee of one monthly minimum wage to the disabled and the elderly aged 65 (sixty-five) or over who prove that they do not have the means to provide for themselves or their family.

§ Paragraph 3 - A family whose monthly **per capita** income is less than 1/4 (one quarter) of the minimum wage is considered unable to provide for the disabled or elderly person.

The first observation refers to the age of 65 as the minimum requirement for obtaining the benefit. In view of the fact that Law 10.741/2003, in its article 1, considered people aged 60 or over to be elderly,

---

24 Available at <http://bolsafamilia10anos.mds.gov.br/themes/bolsa/infografico/superando/superando.html>
25 See also <http://mds.gov.br/assuntos/bolsa-familia/o-que-e/como-funciona>
e<http://www.caixa.gov.br/programas-sociais/bolsa-familia/Paginas/default.aspx> Accessed on 12/02/2016.

a new interpretation of article 20, *caput*, is required in the light of the provisions of the Elderly Statute, i.e. for the purposes of BPC-LOAS the minimum age is 60.

The second consideration has to do with the provisions of Paragraph 3 of Article 20, since it was declared unconstitutional by the Supreme Court[26] when it considered the criterion established by the norm to be outdated for characterizing the situation of miserability in current times and delimiting the amount at ½ minimum wage per person.

The BPC, which is independent of previous contributions, guarantees an income of one monthly minimum wage to the elderly (aged 60 and over) or the physically, intellectually, mentally or sensorially disabled (at any age) when they are unable to prove their own subsistence. The survey found that none of the interviewees claimed to be beneficiaries of the program, 100% answered negatively to the question about receiving BPC-LOAS.

This benefit needs to be publicized through EDH projects in order to reach more and more beneficiaries who meet the requirements of the law, and then it can be expanded to the homeless population.

---

26 Decision in Reclaim (RCL) 4374 of competence of the plenary of the STF. Available at
<http://www.stf.ius.br/nortal/cms/verNoticiaDetalhe.asn?idConteudo=236354>

5 EDUCATIONAL PRODUCT - COURSE PLAN

Human Rights Education Course Plan

The human rights education course will be divided into 4 modules and its priority will be to raise awareness of the need to promote and defend rights.

EMENTA:

MODULE I:

Module I aims to provide initial training in human rights, with an introduction to the main themes of the subject.

1. Fundamentals of Human Rights

2. DH concept

3. Principles of HR

4. DH characteristics

5. Multiple dimensions of HR

6. Generations of DH

7. International Human Rights Protection

7.1   Axes of International Protection

7.2   International protection systems

a.   UN system

b.   OAS system

8. International Documents

8.1   Universal Declaration of Human Rights

8.2   International Covenant on Civil and Political Rights

8.3   International Covenant on Economic, Social and Cultural Rights

8.4   American Convention on Human Rights

8.5   Pact of San Salvador

MODULE II:

The main objective of Module II is to present an exposition of the positive nature of human rights in the Brazilian legal system since the 1988 Constitution.

1. Federal Constitution and Human Rights

2. Foundations, Objectives and Principles of the CRFB/88

3. The Dignity of the Human Person as the core of human rights protection

3.1   Concept

3.2   Features

3.3   Content

4. Fundamental Rights and Guarantees

4.1   Right to life

4.2   Equality

4.3   Freedoms

a.   *Getting around*

b.   *Thinking*

c.   *Expression*

d.   *Collective expression*

e.   *Professional*

4.4   Inviolability

a.   *personality rights*

b.   *home protection*

c.   *secrecy*

4.5   Judicial Guarantees

a.   *Access to justice*

b.   *Right of petition*

c.   *Principle of legality*

d.   *Due process of law*

e.   *Broad defense and adversarial proceedings*

f.   *Presumption of innocence*

g.   *Habeas Corpus*

h.   *Habeas Data*

i.   *Writ of mandamus*

j.   *Injunction*

1.   *Açaopopular*

4.6   Social Rights

a.   *Education*

b.   *Health*

c.   *Social Security*

d.   *Social Assistance*

e.   *Food*

f.   *Housing*

g.   *Transportation*

h.   *Culture and Leisure*

i.   *Security*

j.   *Work*

4.7   Political Rights

-      *Popular sovereignty*

-      *Instruments of direct democracy*

-      *Voter Registration and Voting*

-      *Electoral Systems: Majoritarian and Proportional*

MODULE III

The aim of Module III is to apply the guidelines of EDH to the humanistic formation of the student.

1. EDH concept

2. EDH fundamentals

3. Objectives of EDH

4. Dimensions of EDH

5. National Human Rights Plan-3

6. National Human Rights Education Plan

7. Curriculum Guidelines for EDH

8. Important concepts

9. Human Rights of Minorities and Vulnerable Groups

9.1   Concept of People in Situations of Vulnerability

9.2   Women

9.3   Afro-descendants

9.4   Children and adolescents

9.5   Elderly

9.6   LGBTTIQ group

9.7   Indigenous Peoples

9.8   People with disabilities

9.9   People deprived of their liberty

9.10 Refugees

MODULE IV:

Module 4 aims to address the issues analyzed through the social data obtained in the research, mainly related to public policies for promoting and defending rights.

1. Family Allowance

2. Social Security Benefits

3. Continuous Cash Benefit - LOAS

4. Work and Income

5. Education

6. City Statute

6.1   Morar Carioca Project - Rio de Janeiro City Hall

6.2   My House My Life Program - Federal Government

7. Special Secretariat for Human Rights

7.1   Federal collegiate bodies for the defense of human rights

7.2   Law for all program

8. Access to Justice

8.1   Federal Public Defender's Office (DPU)

8.3   Public Defender's Office of the State of Rio de Janeiro (DPERJ)

8.4   Public Prosecutor's Office (MP-RJ)

9. Human Rights Organizations

6 CONCLUSION

In view of the whole scenario presented in the course of this work, one thing is quite clear: human rights education is a contemporary social necessity. Education needs to be redirected towards the humanist formation of the individual, prioritizing knowledge of rights and the promotion of values such as respect, tolerance, equality, social justice, solidarity and peace. This education, based on the reinforcement of human values, aims to enable the individual to be the protagonist of the process of development as freedom, which precisely aims to expand individual freedoms and capacities, which are determining factors for effective human development. This research was carried out at the Casa do Trabalhador (Workers' House), a public space designed to implement work and income policies at the state government level, located within the Manguinhos community. The work sought to verify the existence of prior knowledge about human rights among the people interviewed, all of whom live in the Manguinhos community, and their interest in acquiring them. Analysis of the data obtained showed that 73.91% of the people interviewed had no knowledge of human rights and 91.30% were interested in acquiring knowledge of the subject. The results show a fertile field for the implementation of human rights education, especially considering the situations of vulnerability to which the inhabitants of Rio de Janeiro's favelas are exposed, as outlined in the development of this work. It is important to show that the idea of creating a course in human rights for one community in Rio de Janeiro opens the way for new projects in different communities. Initially, we propose training based on the legal discipline of human rights in the international sphere, and then contextualize them with the Brazilian Constitution of 1988. In a third stage, the aim is to bring the students closer to the foundations and objectives of human rights education, as well as the values that should form the basis of contemporary political, economic and social relations. Finally, based on the data obtained in the application of the survey instrument, a specific content was drawn up on this information, looking at important issues related to development such as work, education, income, social assistance and the environment. The EDH Course Plan aims to contribute to achieving the fundamental objectives of the Federative Republic of Brazil of building a free, just and supportive society, guaranteeing national development, eradicating poverty and social inequalities and, above all, promoting the good of all, without prejudice to origin, race, sex, color, age or any other form of discrimination.

APPENDIX A - SURVEY INSTRUMENT

POSTGRADUATE PROGRAM IN LOCAL DEVELOPMENT

RESEARCH TOOL: HUMAN RIGHTS EDUCATION IN THE MANGUINHOS COMMUNITY: DEVELOPMENT AS FREEDOM

STUDENT: FERNANDA BALDANZA

*I DECLARE THAT I AM AWARE THAT I WILL BE TAKING PART IN A RESEARCH STUDY AND THAT MY DATA MAY BE USED IN ANY WAY.

BE PUBLISHED: ____

PERSONAL DATA:

NAME:

CPF:

AGE:

GENDER: ( ) MALE ( ) FEMALE

WHERE YOU LIVE:

RACE: ( ) BLACK ( ) WHITE ( ) BROWN

FAMILY

HOW MANY CHILDREN DO YOU HAVE ( ) 0 ( ) 1 ( ) 2

( ) 03   ( ) 0 4 ( ) MORE THAN 4

IS ANYONE IN PRISON IN YOUR FAMILY? ( ) YES ( ) NO

SOCIAL DATA:

MONTHLY INCOME: ( ) UP TO 1 MINIMUM WAGE ( )FROM 1 TO 2 MINIMUM WAGES ( )ABOVE 2

MINIMUM WAGES ( )OVER 3 MINIMUM WAGES

EDUCATION: ( ) 1ST GRADE ( ) INCOMPLETE 1ST GRADE ( ) 2ND GRADE ( ) INCOMPLETE 2ND GRADE ( )

HIGHER ( ) NONE

HOUSING

DO YOU OWN YOUR HOME? ( )YES ( )NO

IS THERE BASIC SANITATION IN YOUR HOUSE AND ON YOUR STREET? ( ) YES ( )NO DO YOU HAVE ( ) A FRIDGE ( ) A TV ( ) AIR CONDITIONING

WORK

( ) EMPLOYED ( ) UNEMPLOYED ( ) SELF-EMPLOYED

( ) RECEIVES UNEMPLOYMENT BENEFITS ( ) HAS ALREADY RECEIVED UNEMPLOYMENT BENEFITS

HEALTH AND LEISURE

DO YOU PLAY SPORT? ( )YES ( )NO

DO YOU GO TO THE DOCTOR REGULARLY? ( ) YES ( )NO

IF FEMALE, DO YOU REGULARLY UNDERGO CANCER PREVENTION? ( ) YES ( )NO

IF MALE, DO YOU TAKE REGULAR CANCER PREVENTION ( ) YES ( )NO

HEALTH AND ENVIRONMENT

IS THERE PIPED WATER FROM CEDAE IN YOUR HOUSE? ( ) YES ( )NO

DOES YOUR COMMUNITY HAVE SELECTIVE WASTE COLLECTION? ( ) YES ( )NO

THE COMLURB TRUCK PASSES BY TO PICK UP THE GARBAGE ( ) YES ( )NO

WHERE DO YOU PUT YOUR GARBAGE? ( ) IN THE GARBAGE CAN   () IN THE STREET ( ) IN THE TRUCK ( )

ASSISTANCE

DO YOU RECEIVE ANY SOCIAL SECURITY BENEFITS? ( )YES ( )NO

do you receive family allowance? ( )yes ( )no

RECEIVES LOAS ( )YES ( )NO

HUMAN RIGHTS:

1)   DO YOU KNOW ABOUT HUMAN RIGHTS? ( )YES ( )NO

2)   ARE YOU INTERESTED IN LEARNING ABOUT HUMAN RIGHTS? ( ) YES ( ) NO

3)   ARE YOU AWARE OF HUMAN RIGHTS PROTECTION BODIES? ( ) YES ( ) NO

4)   ARE YOU INTERESTED IN TAKING A COURSE ON HUMAN RIGHTS? ( ) YES ( ) NO

REASON FOR SEEKING THE WORKER'S HOUSE:

( )LEGAL ASSISTANCE

( )JOB VACANCIES

( )EMPLOYMENT INSURANCE

( )DOCUMENTS AND OTHERS.

REFERENCES

ALVES, José Augusto Lindgren. **The declaration of human rights in** post-modernity, 1999. Available at <http://www.dhnet.org.br/direitos/militantes/lindgrenalves/lindgren 100.htm>

Accessed on 12/06/2016.

AGAMBEN, Giorgio. Homo Sacer: Sovereign Power and Naked Life. Translated by Henrique Burigo. Henrique Burigo. Belo Horizonte: UFMG, 2007.

ANADEP, National Association of Public Defenders. **100 Brasilia Rules for access to justice for people in vulnerable conditions.** XIV Ibero-American Judicial Conference. Brasilia, 2008. Available at <https://www.anadep.org.br/wtksite/100-Regras-de-Brasilia-versao-reduzida.pdf>

ARIAS, G. **In 1953 the structure of DNA was discovered**. Passo Fundo: Embrapa Trigo, 2004 (Embrapa Trigo. Documentos Online; 44). Available at: <http://www.cnpt.embrapa.br/biblio/do/p do44.htm> Accessed on :14/05/16.

ARISTOTLES. **Politics**. Translated by Roberto Leal Ferreira. Sao Paulo: Martins Fontes, 2002.

BARROSO, Luis Roberto. **The Dignity of the Human Person in Contemporary Constitutional Law.** Belo Horizonte: Forum, 2014.

. **The Efficiency and Effectiveness of the Right to Liberty**. In: Revista do Instituto Brasileiro de Direitos Humanos. Year 2, Vol. 2, Number 2, 2001.

BENEDEK, Wolfgang. **Handbook of Human Rights Education.** Translated by Vital Moreira and Carla de Marcelino Gomes (Coord.). European Training and Research Center for Human Rights and Democracy (ETC), Graz, 2012.

BOBBIO, Norberto. **The Age of Rights.** Rio de Janeiro: Elsevier, 2004.

BRAZIL. **Constitution of the Federative Republic of Brazil**. Brasilia: Senate, 1988.

. National Committee for Human Rights Education. **National Plan for Human Rights Education: 2007**. Brasilia: Special Secretariat for Human Rights, 2007.

. Presidency of the Republic. **Lei de Diretrizes e Bases da Educaçao Nacional** - LDB, Brasilia: MEC, 1996.

. Presidency of the Republic. **National Education Plan**. Law 13.005/14. Brasilia: PR, 2014.

. Special Secretariat for Human Rights of the Presidency of the Republic. **National Human Rights Program (PNDH-3)**. Rev. ed. Brasilia: SEDH/PR, 2010.

. **Guiding text for the elaboration of the National Guidelines for Human Rights Education.** Brasilia: National Education Council, 2011.

. MEC. **National Guidelines for Human Rights Education**. National Education Council. Resolution No. 1/12. Brasilia: MEC, 2012.

. MEC. National Education   Council. **National Curricular Guidelines for Bachelor's Degrees.** Resolution n 02/2015. Brasilia: MEC, 2015.

. **Subnormal Agglomerations.** IBGE, 2010. Available at

<http://www.ibge.gov.br/home/presidencia/noticias/imprensa/ppts/00000015164811202 013480105748802.pdf> Acesso em 08/06/2016.

. Secretariat for Human Rights of the Presidency of the Republic (SDH). **Caderno de Educaçao em Direitos Humanos. Human Rights Education: National Guidelines** - Brasilia: General Coordination of Education in SDH/PR, Human Rights, National Secretariat for the Promotion and Defense of Human Rights, 2013.

. National Committee for Human Rights Education. **National Plan for Human Rights Education / National Committee for Human Rights Education. -** Brasilia: Special Secretariat for Human Rights, Ministry of Education, Ministry of Justice, UNESCO, 2007. Available at http://portal.mec.gov.br/index.php?option=com   docman&view=download&alias=2191-   plano-nacional-pdf&category slug=dezembro-2009-pdf&Itemid=30192 Accessed on 13/06/2016.

.PORTAL BRASIL. CITIZENSHIP AND JUSTICE. **Government carries out research into the implementation of the National Human Rights Education Plan.** Published on 29/07/2011. Available at <http://www.brasil.gov.br/cidadania-e- justica/2011/07/government-conducts-research-on-implementation-of-the-national-plan-for-education-in-human-rights> Accessed on 03/06/2016.

. STF. **The Constitution and the Supreme Court.** 4ª ed. Brasilia: Secretaria de Documentaçao, 2011.

BENEVIDES, Maria Vitoria**. Human Rights Education: what is it all about?** Opening lecture of the Seminar on Human Rights Education, Sao Paulo, 18/02/2000. Available at <http://hottopos.com/convenit6/victoria.htm> Accessed on 29/06/2016.

. **Faith in the struggle: the Justice and Peace Commission of Sao Paulo, from dictatorship to democratization**. Sao Paulo: Lettera, 2009.

BONAVIDES, Paulo. **Course in Constitutional Law.** 10. ed. Sao Paulo: Malheiros, 2000.

CANÇADO TRINDADE, Antônio Augusto. Towards an account of the drafting of the Vienna Declaration and Program of Action. **"Balanço dos resultados da Conferência Mundial dos**

Direitos Humanos: Viena, 1993". Revista Brasileira de Politica Internacional n. 36, 1993, pp. 9-27.

. **The humanization of international law.** Belo Horizonte: Del Rey, 2015.

CANDAU, V. **Human rights: challenges for the 21st century**. In: Educaçao em direitos humanos: Fundamentos teórico-metodológicos / Rosa Maria Godoy Silveira, et al. - Joao Pessoa: Editora Universitària, 2007.

COMPARATO, F.K. **A Afirmaçao histórica dos Direitos Humanos**. Sao Paulo: Saraiva, 2003.

. **Foundations of Human Rights**. Sao Paulo: Saraiva, 1997.

COUTINHO, Diogo R. **Direito, Desigualdade e Desenvolvimento**. Sao Paulo: Saraiva, 2013.

DARWIN, C. **The Origin of Species.** Translation of the original 6th edition and last revised by Darwin: The Origin of Species by Means of Natural Selection, or the Preservation of Favoured Races in the Struggle for Life. 6th Edition, with additions and corrections to 1872. John Murray, Albermarle Street, London, 1876. Original first edition: November 24, 1859. Available at <u>http://darwin-online.org.uk/converted/pdf/2009 OriginPortuguese F2062.7.pdf</u> Accessed on 15/06/2016.

. *The descent of man and selection in relation to sex*. London: John Murray, 1871. Available at <http://darwin-online.org.uk/> Accessed on 14/05/16.

DIAS, Clarence. **Human Rights Education as a Strategy for Development.** In: Human Rights Education for the 21st Century. Organized by George J. Andreopoulos; Richard Pierre Claude; translated by Ana Luiza Pinheiro. Sao Paulo: Edusp: Nùcleo de Estudos da Violência, 2007.

ERICKSON, et at. **History of anthropological theory.** Translated by Marcus Penchel. Petrópolis, RJ: Vozes, 2015.

FREIRE, Paulo. **Education as the Practice of Freedom.** Rio de Janeiro: Editora Paz e Terra, 1967.

. **Pedagogy of the Oppressed**. Rio de Janeiro: Editora Paz e Terra, 2014.

HUMAN RIGHTS. **A brief history of human rights.** Available at <http://www.humanrights.com/pt/what-are-human-rights/brief-history/cyrus-cylinder.html> Accessed on 27/05/2016.

JASPERS, Karl. **Introduction to Philosophical Thought.** Translated by Leonidas Hegenberg and Octanny Silveira da Mota. Sao Paulo: Cultrix, 1965 (original work).

MAZZUOLI, Valério. **Course in Human Rights.** Rio de Janeiro: Forense; Sao Paulo: MÉTODO, 2015.

MEIRELLES, Renato. **A country called Favela: the largest survey ever carried out on the Brazilian favela.** Sao Paulo: Editora Gente, 2014.

MICHAELIS online. **Dictionary of the Portuguese Language.** Available at <http://michaelis.uol.com.br/> Accessed on 13/06/2016.

ORGANIZATION OF AMERICAN STATES (OEA). **Pact** *of San José de Costa Rica*. San José: Inter-American Specialized Conference on Human Rights, 1969.

UN. **Universal Declaration of Human Rights**. UN General Assembly:

Paris, France, 1948. Available at <http://www.dudh.org.br/wp-content/uploads/2014/12/dudh.pdf> Accessed on 25/06/2016.

. **UN Charter.** San Francisco, 1945. Available at <http://unicrio.org.br/img/CartadaONU VersoInternet.pdf> Accessed on 13/06/2016.

. World Conference on Human Rights. **Declaration and Program of Action   of Vienna.** Vienna, 1993.   Available   at: <http://www.dhnet.org.br/direitos/anthist/viena/declaracao viena.htm> Accessed on 1/11/15.

. **International Covenant on Civil and Political Rights (ICCPR)**. Geneva: UN, 1966. Available at <http://www.gddc.pt/direitos-humanos/textos-internacionais-   dh/tidhuniversal/cidh-dudh-civil-rights.html> Accessed on 12/06/2016.

. **International Covenant on Economic, Social and Cultural Rights (ICESCR)**. Geneva: UN, 1966. Available at **<http://www.unfpa.org.br/Arquivos/pacto international.pdf> Accessed on 15/11/15.**

. Decade for Human Rights Education (1995-2004). **International Action Plan for the United Nations Decade for Human Rights Education**. Geneva: UN, 1995. Available at <http://www.gddc.pt/direitos- humanos/serie decada 1 b.pdfAccessed on 17/11/15.

. United Nations Declaration on Human Rights Education and Training. **Resolution 66/137. UNGA, 2012.**

. Declaration on the Right to Development. **UNGA: New York, 1986.**

. United Nations Framework Convention on Climate Change. **New York, 1992.**

. World Humanitarian Summit. **Agenda for Humanity**. UNGA: Istanbul, 2016. Available at <https://consultations2.worldhumanitariansummit.org/bitcache/e49881ca33e3740b5f37 162857cedc92c7c1e354?vid=569103&disposition=inline&op=view> Accessed on 13/02/2016.

PALMA, R. F. **History of Law**. Sao Paulo: Saraiva, 2011.

PIOVESAN, Flâvia. **Human Rights and International Constitutional Law.** Sao Paulo: Saraiva, 2013.

PEQUENO, Marconi. **The foundation of human rights**. Human Rights Education: historical-philosophical foundations. Available at

<http://www.dhnet.org.br/dados/cursos/edh/redh/01/02   marconi   pequeno   fundamento dh.pdf>Accessed on: May 14, 2016.

RAMOS, André de Carvalho. **Human Rights Course**. Sao Paulo: Saraiva, 2014.

SARMENTO, Daniel. **The dignity of the human person: content, trajectories and methodology.** Belo Horizonte: Editora Fórum, 2016.

SARLET, Ingo Wolfgang. **Human Dignity and Fundamental Rights in the 1988 Federal Constitution.** Porto Alegre: Livraria do Advogado Editora, 2015.

SEN, Amartya. **Development as Freedom.** Translated by Laura Teixeira Motta; technical review by Ricardo Doninelli Mendes. Sao Paulo: Companhia das Letras, 2010.

SINGER, Peter. **Practical Ethics.** Lisbon: Gradiva, 1993.

TOSI, Giuseppe (org). **Human Rights: History, Theory and Practice.** Joao Pessoa: Editora UFPB, 2004.

UNESCO. **World Program for Human Rights Education - Action Plan**

Phase   One.   New   York   and   Geneva,   2006.   Available   at <http://www.dhnet.org.br/dados/textos/edh/br/plano action world program edh en.p df> Accessed on 13/06/2016.

. **PMEDH - Second Phase Action Plan.** Brasilia: MEC,   2012.   Available   at <http://unesdoc.unesco.org/images/0021/002173/217350por.pdf> Accessed on 18/11/15.

. **PMEDH - Third Phase Action Plan.** Brasilia: MEC,   2015.   Available   at <http://unesdoc.unesco.org/images/0023/002329/232922POR.pdf> Accessed on 13/06/2016.

. **Universal Declaration on the Human Genome and Human Rights.**

UNGA: Paris, 1997. Available at

<http://unesdoc.unesco.org/images/0012/001229/ 122990por.pdf> Accessed on 13/06/2016.

VALLADARES, Licia do Prado. **The invention of the favela.** Rio de Janeiro: Editora FGV, 2005.

VIANNA, C.E.S. **Historical evolution of the concept of education and the constitutional objectives of Brazilian education**, 2006.

Printed by Books on Demand GmbH, Norderstedt / Germany